Classic PATHFINDER

3

Inspiring performance: focus on drama and song

JUDITH HAMILTON, ANNE MCLEOD
& STEVEN FAWKES

WITH CONTRIBUTIONS FROM JANET LLOYD & KHEYA MAIR

CiLT The National Centre for Languages

The views expressed in this publication are the authors' and do not necessarily represent those of CILT.

Acknowledgements

The photos in Part 1 show pupils from Queensferry High School, South Queensferry, Scotland. We would like to thank Raymond Simpson, PT Computing, for taking the photos. *Judith Hamilton and Anne McLeod*

For their encouragement in the many stages of development of this project I would like to thank the following colleagues and friends: Jenifer Alison, Clare Hoogewerf, Stella Marsh, Valerie Miller, Derek Neil, Angela Nichols, Ann Swarbrick, Doreen Smith, Goldenhill Methodist Chapel, all the pupils and colleagues with whom the song activities were developed, and all at CILT. *Steven Fawkes*

This compilation first published 2003 by the Centre for Information on Language Teaching and Research (CILT), 20 Bedfordbury, London WC2N 4LB

ISBN 1 904243 10 X

A catalogue record for this book is available from the British Library

Printed in Great Britain by Hobbs

CILT Publications are available from: **Central Books,** 99 Wallis Rd, London E9 5LN. Tel: 0845 458 9910. Fax: 0845 458 9912. On-line ordering: www.centralbooks.co.uk. Book trade representation (UK and Ireland): **Broadcast Book Services,** Charter House, 29a London Road, Croydon CR0 2RE. Tel: 020 8681 8949. Fax: 020 8688 0615.

Contents

Part 2
With a song in my scheme of work   39

Foreword

As languages teachers we are the most fortunate of teachers – all subjects are ours. Whatever the children want to communicate about, whatever they want to read about, is our subject matter. (Rivers 1972: 68)

Learning activities in the languages classroom need to be devised to show that languages are not just about assimilating the rules of a grammatical system but also to demonstrate to pupils that they are a code of communication through which they can access different cultures, different attitudes, different ways of thinking and doing. Languages are not so much classroom subjects as ever-malleable tools through which people say, read, write, sing what they want. Rivers wrote the statement above over thirty years ago and it still has resonance for us today. This is not to suggest that we go round in continual circles, making scant progress as we go, but that ideas rooted in research about the needs of language learners are those which endure. Some ideas are more than worth revisiting within the context of the initiative-packed modern world of education in which we live. In this book we have brought together two publications, first individually published as *Pathfinders,* brimming with creative teaching ideas which encourage teachers and pupils alike to see language very much as a means of effective communication. They have been up-dated and enhanced by the authors in the light of developments in MFL education since they were first published. We have packaged the two publications within this one book because of the clear links between them in terms of presenting ideas for getting pupils to use their imagination while learning a new language. Both books:

- encourage teachers to be inventive;
- describe ideas which are easily achievable in normal classrooms;
- encourage pupils to think creatively through structured activities;
- break from the norm.

Within this new publication you will find a clear rationale for using both drama and song to encourage linguistic development.

Judith Hamilton and **Anne McLeod** have worked with their drama teaching colleague Sandra McLellan to adapt drama-based activities for the languages classroom, focusing particularly on ideas for getting pupils talking and moving and thinking creatively. In Part 1 the authors encourage teachers to experiment with different pupil groupings and give clear descriptions of ways of managing the classroom and pupil learning. They outline ideas for using simulation, improvisation and creative role play for classes of different ages and at different levels of attainment. Drama, of course, has its own conventions and pupils' expectations are very different in drama from their expectations of a languages lesson. The authors give useful tips on getting started and explain some of the more common drama techniques which are adaptable for our MFL classrooms.

Janet Lloyd contributes a case study which brings the world of art into the languages classroom to stimulate learners' creativity, providing a basis for language production at a variety of levels.

Steven Fawkes is an expert at exploiting song in the languages classroom and in Part 2 you will find ideas on the sort of songs you may want to use with your classes. He analyses how songs support learning by cleverly categorising his ideas under such headings as a song for pronunciation, a song for sorting, a song for note-taking, etc. He also acknowledges that MFL teachers can be extremely creative thinkers and gives us some tips for composing our own songs for our pupils.

Kheya Mair contributes a case study which demonstrates clearly how she builds songs into her everyday classroom routine rather than using them as a one-off teaching idea.

We have lived through many initiatives since the first publication of these books, but the needs of language learners have not changed. They need more than ever frequent opportunities to use the language in a way that demonstrates to them that it is a tool which they can manipulate to say, write, do what they want. The ideas in this book illustrate achievable ways of presenting such opportunities through drama and song. We think you'll enjoy reading about them and we hope they inspire you to experiment in your own classroom.

Ann Swarbrick
Language Teaching Adviser, CILT

Rivers, W.M. (1972) *Speaking in many tongues: essays in foreign language teaching.* Rowley, Mass.: Newbury House.

Part 1

Drama in the languages classroom

JUDITH HAMILTON & ANNE MCLEOD

WITH A CONTRIBUTION BY JANET LLOYD

Introduction

Language teachers have over the years shown an increasing interest in the experiences of their colleagues in drama departments. This book intends to support, encourage and inform teachers of foreign languages who are already involved or who would like to get involved in this area. The authors have worked in the same department together with their colleague, the Principal Teacher of Drama, Sandra McLellan, who helped them to develop their own skills and materials.

Drama has a great deal to offer language teachers. Both subjects want learners to be:

- active participants;
- willing communicators;
- responsible;
- flexible;
- open-minded;

and to be able to:

- develop and transfer the skills they acquire in one set of circumstances to another, different set of circumstances.

1   Why should I do it?

DRAMA IS ABOUT MAKING REAL MEANINGS

Much has been written about what is communicative or not in language teaching and perhaps no term is so widely misused as 'communication'. One of the critical factors for determining how communicative any language activity is, is to ask the question 'Would it occur naturally in the mother tongue under these circumstances?'. Much of what we say in language classrooms is denuded of any real meaning and is only tolerable because we do **not** say it in the mother tongue.

How are we to offer our learners the scope for 'learning how to mean', to adopt a phrase of Michael Halliday's, while at the same time keeping the level of difficulty to one at which they can happily cope and feel encouraged? How can we use the target language to make real meanings **in** the language rather than to talk **about** the language? Drama offers us the context in which to do this.

WHERE DRAMA TECHNIQUES AND LANGUAGE TEACHING MEET

The use of drama techniques fits naturally into the theoretical context of studies into the nature of language and language learning. Language teachers have over the years been offered many theories which would supposedly enhance, or perhaps even transform their teaching. Some of these have turned out to be at best irrelevant distractions. Yet all teachers operate on the basis of 'theories' of one kind or another, consciously or unconsciously. They come from a variety of sources and are often referred to as 'beliefs'. When the findings/recommendations of researchers go against our 'beliefs', and especially when they nevertheless influence, as some of them do, national policy and hence our work in the classroom, the tendency is to reject 'theory' as a whole, especially since many teachers remember only too well the results of the implementation of some of the more bizarre of these. All the more reason therefore for us as practitioners to examine, analyse and evaluate our own teaching practice. All good teachers are action researchers in their classrooms.

One of the principal concerns at the moment is to find ways of creating for our pupils a more natural language learning environment. We know that the classroom is not the best place to get to grips with a foreign language. Given the chance, we would opt for having our pupils live in the foreign language community and dispense with our services altogether. Because we know that two weeks living with a foreign family is probably worth a year of our teaching, we try as much as possible to recreate such an experience in our classroom with posters, realia and sounds that reflect this, increasingly using the target language ourselves, encouraging our pupils to say what they mean in the language and correcting for the most part only those errors that impede communication. We no longer simply **describe** the rules of the language; we are concerned with having our pupils **perform** in the language. Yet we know that this performance is not something wholly within our control, not something we can force from unwilling pupils. There has to be a reason, a context, the motivation or need to use the language. It is in the creation of such contexts for communication that drama techniques have such a strong claim on our attention.

THE METHODOLOGICAL CONTINUUM

We have attempted in this diagram to represent a rationale for those who are considering using drama techniques. It should be clear from this how drama techniques might play a useful role whatever a teacher's personal *point de départ*.

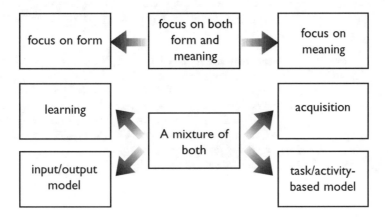

I teach/present the structure, my pupils learn through imitation and practice.	I like to create the need for my pupils to use a particular structure and at the same time encourage the building up of their own internalised grammar system.	My pupils are taught to be resourceful and to find within themselves, using a variety of sources and strategies, a way of meeting their linguistic needs.

No matter what kind of teacher you are or whereabouts on the continuum you would place yourself, drama still has something to offer.

I am a traditional teacher

I believe in teaching structures and grammar. I want my students to practise 'mon/ma/mes', 'son/sa/ses'.

I can use the **Circle memory game** (see p12) and focus on the following structures.

Student A: *J'ai perdu **mon** passeport.*

Student B: *Elle a perdu **son** passeport. Moi, j'ai perdu **mes** clefs.*

Student C: *Elle a perdu **son** passeport. Il a perdu **ses** clefs. Moi, j'ai perdu **ma** bague.*

I want the best of both worlds

I have a structure in mind, but I believe that pupils can best learn this in a **meaningful situation** through a **meaningful activity**. For example:

J'ai perdu …
Il/Elle a perdu …

I can use the **Circle memory game**. I am not primarily interested in 'mon/ma/mes'. I am more interested in words which carry meaning (i.e. nouns and pronouns). The game creates the need for students to use the correct *'il/elle'* pronoun. From the students' point of view, calling a girl *'il'* is 'wrong' and they actually feel it, because the person referred to, as well as the rest of the class, will react to the mistake. The need to get this right is created by the **game** and not by me as teacher. The game gives students a meaningful context for saying *'J'ai perdu …'* etc.

I am a 'humanistic' teacher

I believe in experiential learning and the development of the individual.

I want to create an atmosphere conducive to communication in which my pupils only ever use language where they actually 'mean' in the Halliday sense.

My pupils acquire a given structure **because** it, or something very like it, comes up as we go along.

I would use the **Circle memory game** because it is a way of making students feel good about themselves – they really can recall a great deal. This way they learn to help each other. Whether I decide to do it with *'J'ai perdu …'* or with *'J'aime …'* or *'Je suis allé à …'* is neither here nor there. It's the experience of success and co-operation that counts.

DRAMA ENCOURAGES PUPIL TALK

Given the importance of talk in our classrooms, it is vital to create an atmosphere in which the learners are not afraid to open their mouths and speak in the target language. This kind of stress-free, fun teaching encourages pupils to participate without embarrassment since the emphasis on completing the task in hand distracts the learner from the language and focuses their attention firmly on this task – i.e. they stop worrying 'Help, she's going to ask me to say something in French' , because what they want to do is participate in the activity. Drama is a way of building confidence and often succeeds where other methods have failed.

It is hard to imagine anything else that offers to language teachers such a wide variety of types of talk, e.g. monologues, paired speaking, role plays, group discussions, reporting, talking in response to other stimuli, problem-solving, developing scenarios, acting out, etc. From explaining, complaining, praising, disagreeing to exhorting, apologising and requesting – there is no language function that drama is not capable of easily encompassing.

DRAMA AND THE DEVELOPMENT OF THE INDIVIDUAL

As methodology has changed over recent years towards more active production of the foreign language, there has been a tendency for language teachers to regard learners as principally 'talking heads'. Drama on the other hand involves the whole person intellectually, physically and emotionally. It can lead, through the exploration of unknown or familiar situations, to insights about the self as well as other people, situations and places. Involving relations with others, it promotes social and adaptive skills which in their turn feed into the process of learning a foreign language. It allows for dealing with sensitive issues such as gender, race and conflicts in a sensitive and non-threatening way. Learners are encouraged to explore themselves and their reactions in relation to the outside world in a way which can be both strengthening and enriching.

USE ACROSS THE ABILITY RANGE

The experiences offered in drama lend themselves very much to use with different year groups and to differentiation within the classroom. The activities can be as demanding or undemanding linguistically as the teacher chooses, and the atmosphere should always be a non-threatening one in which all learners feel able to contribute something.

Once teachers have mastered a few essential techniques, they are able to adapt them for use with learners of different levels of ability. For example, the *Circle memory game* (see p12) can easily be used to practise structures at different levels, as can the *'Paul Jones' double circle* (p17), the *Find a partner technique* (p27) and many others. Drama activities can offer just as much to senior classes as to junior classes in terms of providing a context for language acquisition and a reason to use the target language in a meaningful way.

Learners who have difficulty accessing a more traditionally delivered curriculum have also much to gain from taking part in drama. Lots of the activities described under 'Movement' (see p22) and 'Mime' (see p23) require the students to listen to the target language and respond in some way other than in speech. Many students with learning difficulties find the production of language very hard and can feel scared or even intimidated when asked to speak in front of more confident classmates. 'Movement and mime' activities serve as a kind of camouflage for these students, allowing them to join in with the rest of the class without the risk of embarrassment. Moreover, not having to respond through speech in the target language offers everyone a level playing field and the chance to make a valuable contribution. And it's fun!

Of course this exposure to non-threatening activities is likely also to be beneficial in terms of developing listening skills and language acquisition in general. It may even encourage learners to have a go at speaking the language in situations where they are not made to stand out. Not only can the least confident learners achieve something worthwhile in the language class, they may also actually enjoy the experience.

2 Can I do it?

 SOME POPULAR MISCONCEPTIONS

Drama means:

- kids hanging from the lights;
- noise and chaos;
- lots of sketches;
- horrendous discipline problems;
- you have to write a thousand role play cards;
- you have to have a talent for mime;
- no written work;
- embarrassing activities to do with touching people;
- you need small practical set classes;
- more action than talk;
- an unacceptable amount of errors;
- kids moving about all over the place;
- you can't do it in the average classroom;
- it's only a special type of teacher who can cope.

ON THE CONTRARY

Using drama techniques can mean:

- learners doing a fair amount of silent reading;
- periods of quiet reflection;
- an atmosphere of concentration;
- learners co-operating to encourage good behaviour;
- an absence of discipline problems caused by bored, unmotivated learners;
- the blossoming of a previously silent and unco-operative pupil;
- learners working at their desks in their own classroom;
- the whole class listening to the teacher;
- the whole class silently watching a group perform;
- more work covered than the teacher ever deemed possible;
- learners using the target language willingly and without inhibition.

You don't have to be an energetic, extrovert person to use drama techniques successfully in your classroom. Drama techniques can be successfully used by anyone, regardless of personality. Remember that drama is a **way of thinking** about teaching and learning. The trick is to stop thinking of yourself as a teacher of languages and to start thinking of yourself as a teacher of something **through** languages – a teacher of people, not a teacher of nouns, verbs, etc.

3 Essential techniques – all ages and levels

Once you have mastered a few basic techniques you will find yourself able to use them in a whole variety of ways with a whole variety of structures.

THE CIRCLE WHERE EVERYONE REMAINS SEATED

The circle where everyone remains seated

Memory games

(Otherwise known as *I went to the market and I bought … or In my grandmother's suitcase …*)

Basic technique

One student says what they bought. Next student repeats first student's item and adds one of their own. All students listen carefully, as they will have to remember all the preceding items before adding their own. There must be no repetition of a previously mentioned item.

Varieties

- *With real objects*
  Fill a carrier bag with items most of which the students know already in the target language

(e.g. classroom objects) or for which the word is identical or similar to English (e.g. *orange, banane, lion*). Student A removes an object and names it in the target language, student B takes an object, names the previous object and the one he or she has taken, and so on.

Using real objects lends interest to practising a whole variety of structures from *J'ai acheté, Je voudrais* to *J'aurais dû acheter* and *Ich hätte … nicht vergessen sollen* (plus accusative!).

* *Practising structures at different levels*

Beginners	Student A:	*J'adore Tom Cruise.*
	Student B:	*Elle adore Tom Cruise. Moi, j'adore le foot* etc.
Intermediate	Student A:	*Le weekend, je suis allé au cinéma.*
	Student B:	*Le weekend, il est allé au cinéma, et moi, j'ai regardé la télé* etc.
Advanced	Student A:	*Ich habe Angst, wenn ich allein bin.*
	Student B:	*Er hat Angst, wenn er allein ist, und ich habe Angst vor Spinnen* etc.

Circular conversations

Student A:	*Bonjour. Comment ça va?*
Student B:	*Très bien, merci. Et toi?*
Student C:	*Moi, ça ne va pas.*
Student D:	*Tu as un problème?*
Student E:	*Oui. J'ai oublié mes devoirs.*
Student F:	*Quels devoirs?* etc

This can clearly be done at any level. Once learners have got the idea, they become very adept at it.

Circular stories

Another variety is to use this technique to tell a story. This can be started by using a prompt card, by the teacher, or by an inventive learner.

Pass the parcel

Just like the party game, but using different sized envelopes. The music stops. The student opens the large envelope. Stuck on the envelope inside is one of the following:

* a number to be read aloud;
* a picture of a sport/activity/animal/musical instrument etc to be mimed for the rest of the class to guess using the target language;
* an instruction for a student to carry out;
* any ideas of your own!

Students carry out the task. Music starts again. When it stops, next student opens envelope etc.

 ## THE CIRCLE WHERE PEOPLE MOVE IN ORDER TO FIND A SEAT

Do you like your neighbour?

Student A stands in the middle of the circle. Other students are all seated. The object of the activity is to find a seat. Student A asks a question of any student in the circle. The question should require a yes/no answer. For example: *Tu aimes ton voisin? Magst du Eis?* If the student's reply is 'yes', then everyone remains seated and student A continues to ask the question of other students. If the reply is 'no', then every student in the circle must change their seat as quickly as possible. In their new seat they must not be sitting beside either of their previous 'neighbours'. Student A must also try to find a seat. There will be one person left without a chair. This person continues to ask questions as before, and the same procedure is followed for changing seats. Speed is an important factor in the success of this activity.

Do you like your neighbour?

This activity is useful as a warm-up to more complicated tasks, or in its own right as a means of practising questions. The same question, chosen by the teacher, may be asked by every student, or the activity can be made more open-ended by allowing the students to choose their own questions.

Movement by numbers

Basic technique

Teacher allocates the numbers 1–4/5 to individual students all round the circle, so that there are several 1's, 2's, 3's, etc. He or she calls out a number and the students who have been given this number stand up and change seats as quickly as possible. The teacher must also try to find a seat. One person will be left in the middle and must call out another number between 1 and 4/5, and the same procedure is followed for changing and finding seats. Speed is essential (but safety is also important!).

The circle where people move in order to find a seat

Varieties

• Instead of numbers, the teacher allocates other items such as letters of the alphabet, pets, sports, colours, etc.

• In this variety it is possible for everyone to change seats at once. For example *Fruit salad*:

Teacher allocates the names of 4–6 fruits to students in the circle. Students change seats when their fruit is called. In addition, when *Fruit salad* is called out, **all** students must stand up and change seats.

Other ideas

Teacher allocates animals, all change on 'zoo'; teacher allocates facial features, all change on 'face'; teacher allocates colours, all change on 'rainbow', etc.

• A further variation would be to hand out pictures of the items to the students. Once everyone has changed seats, students should pass their card to the person on their right before the next item is called out. This tests students' knowledge of various vocabulary items in the course of the activity.

• Movement with mime. As above, but pupils must mime as they move, e.g. playing tennis, kicking a football, etc. You can also do this with the adjectives of mood: *terrifié, fatigué*, etc. On the call *Crise de nerfs*, all students move, miming their mood as they go.

Movement with mime

Banana, banana, banana

Basic technique

Every student is given the name of a different fruit or vegetable. The teacher stands in the centre of the circle and calls out the name of one fruit/vegetable three times, as quickly as possible. The student who has been given the name of this fruit/vegetable must shout it out once, before the teacher has called it out three times. If the student succeeds, she keeps her seat. If not, she must give up her seat to the person in the middle.

Varieties

- Other vocabulary areas may be chosen, e.g. sport and hobbies, school subjects, household objects, classroom objects, animals, Christmas presents, clothes, etc.

- Students are given a card with a picture of the item. (Each student must be given a different card.) Proceed as above, but now and again the teacher asks students to pass the card to the person on their right/left.

Handing out cards

THE 'PAUL JONES' DOUBLE CIRCLE

Basic technique

You need:

- Inner circle facing out

- Outer circle facing in – same number in each so each student has a
partner (see photo below)
(Students may be seated or standing)

You give a task to the whole group. They carry this out. You then tell one circle (e.g. the outer
one) to move to their left or right. Thus each person has a new partner. You repeat the task
(or give another task). The changing of partners continues until the end of the exercise. This
offers an endless variety of opportunities for speaking at all levels. Some are listed below.

The 'Paul Jones' double circle

You can:
- practise basic structures:
  - ask your partner where she lives;
  - ask your partner what he got for Christmas;
  - talk to your partner about how you both spent the weekend;
  - talk about what you would each do if you had £1,000.

- cover a variety of topics – talk about:
  - the weather;
  - your likes/dislikes at school;
  - your pets;
  - yesterday's TV programmes;
  - your favourite food etc.

- or give more challenging topics:
  - feminism;
  - the death penalty;
  - environmental pollution;
  - how to improve conditions for pupils in your year group.

- include movement:
  - put your hand on your partner's head and wish her/him Merry Christmas;
  - stand back to back and talk about the weather.

- use it for mime on its own:
  - you are playing tennis;
  - you are playing a duet on the piano.

- use it for mime and talk:
  - you are setting the table – discuss what's for tea;
  - you are eating spaghetti – talk about your holiday in Italy.

- use it with cue cards:
  - lost property – a selection of pictures of lost objects, time and place lost on the card (sufficient to have one card per pair). Pupils are in the Lost Property Office and must build a conversation round the pictures (see illustration).
  - holidays – pictures of hotel, weather, means of transport

Cue cards: lost property

THE CHAIN

Basic technique

One large circle but students start in pairs facing their partners.

This is similar to the 'Paul Jones' but leads to a tighter circle which can be less inhibiting and is good as a warm-up.

The teacher chooses a structure which students will use throughout the activity. This should initially be very simple – e.g. Student A: *Bonjour, ça va?* Student B: *Ça va bien, merci.*

However, they have to say this to each other while carrying out another instruction:

e.g.   Greet your partner and jump up and down five times.

The students facing in one direction now move on to their next partner as in the 'chain' in the eightsome reel. A further instruction is given:

e.g.   Greet your partner and put both hands on your head.

The movements to be carried out can become increasingly complex: 'Put your right hand on your partner's left shoulder and your left hand on her/his knee/foot and greet her/him'.

It is fun to get partners to stand back to back and call their 'conversation' over their heads to each other at the end.

'Paul Jones' – touch head (can also be done in a chain)

BEATING TIME TECHNIQUES

Basic technique

This activity is best done seated in a circle. The teacher sets up a rhythm by, for example, tapping her knees twice then snapping her fingers once, pausing, before continuing the rhythm, to allow for something to be said in the gap. Pupils speak in turn around the circle, without repeating what anyone else has already said.

Varieties

• Pupils say anything at all in the target language.

• A topic is chosen (e.g. animals, food, sports, etc) and pupils must name in the target language items which come under this heading.

• Numbers – straight counting.

• Numbers – counting backwards.

- Counting up in odd/even numbers.

- Counting up in 5's, 4's, etc.

- Alphabet forwards and backwards.

- Each new word must begin with the last letter of the previous word (e.g. *lait, thé*, etc).

- Word association – Teacher gives a word (e.g. school). Each student in turn must give a word in the target language which he associates with the school (e.g. homework, teacher, etc).

- Word association – Teacher gives a word (e.g. school). A student gives a word which he associates with this (e.g. pencil). Next student gives a word he associates with the previous word (e.g. wood), and so on.

If a student fails to say anything when it is his turn, or repeats an item that someone else has already said, he should stand up, and at the end of the 'round' be given a forfeit (e.g. dance the Highland Fling, do the Twist in slow motion, etc.)

Beating time – slap knees

Follow up

This activity can also be made into a memory game. Students must try to remember what other students said. Teacher can then point to a particular student and ask the rest of the group what he said, or teacher can ask one student to go round the circle trying to remember what each of the other students said.

Tip

The teacher should lead the time-beating and students should be asked to follow his/her lead and beat in time with the teacher. If not, the beat gets faster and faster and there is not enough time for each student to speak.

MOVEMENT

We are starting with movement because it is easier than mime! If you have never asked your students to move out from behind their desks, do not assume that they will be able to move around safely or sensibly! Students must be taught how to move around the classroom in an acceptable manner (or the maths department downstairs will complain!)

'Bring me something ...'

Students are divided into teams. Teacher calls out 'Bring me something red/round/made of wood/etc'. The first team to produce a suitable item wins the point.

'Bring me something you could use to ...'

Teacher calls out as before, e.g. 'something you could use to stir your tea'. Each team must find a suitable object and mime the activity (e.g. stirring tea with a pencil).

Commands

This can be done whole class, in teams, in named groups:

e.g. • Blue group, put your hands on your heads.
 • Green group, pick up the telephone.
 • Team A, sit on the floor.
 • Team B, form a circle, etc.

Simon says

'Do this if ...'

e.g. • Stand up if you like cheese.
 • Stand up and jump up and down if you have long hair.
 • Stand up on one leg if you saw *Eastenders* last night.
 • Pull your right ear if you want to go home.
 • Change seats if your surname begins with B, etc.

Moving furniture

Teacher issues instructions

e.g. • Make your area of the classroom into a train compartment:
 • Make your area of the classroom into a room in a house.
 • Make your area of the classroom into a restaurant.
 • Make your area of the classroom into a pet shop.
 • Make your area of the classroom into a hospital ward, etc.

An extension of this activity would be to have a suitable conversation in the space created.

Team game

One team member stands at the front of the classroom facing the board and blindfolded. The teacher points to one person in the opposing team. On the word 'Go' they try to reach the board before the blindfolded person points in their direction. If they fail to reach the board, the blindfolded person gives them a task, e.g. count up to ten. If they reach the board, they get the blindfold and a team point.

The birthday line

Students are asked to make one long line starting with the people whose birthdays fall in January and ending with those whose birthdays are in December. Once they are in the correct place for the months, they sort themselves out in order of the date of the month as well. This can lead on to other words on the birthday theme or indeed into horoscopes, where the dividing line is not the calendar month but the horoscope group.

 # MIME

This may seem a daunting area for a non-drama specialist, but you can build up from simple, warm-up mime activities to activities which demand good co-ordination and observation on the part of the learners. If your school has a drama specialist, get help – it makes all the difference.

Don't assume that a mime activity means no foreign language production from the students. While mime is an excellent vehicle for 'listen and do' activities, students can also be asked to respond orally to mimes done by others in the class, as in 'miming and guessing' games.

Listen/read and mime

Numbers

Individual students are asked to form the shape of a number (1–9) with their body, or pairs of students are asked to form the shape of two-digit numbers. This can either be a 'listen and do' activity, where the teacher calls out a number in the target language for the students to mime, or it can be a guessing game, where students choose their own numbers to be guessed by the rest of the class in the target language.

Alphabet

As above, but forming letters of the alphabet. Groups of students can be asked to form whole words.

Shapes and sizes

As above, but students individually, in pairs, or in groups must form shapes and sizes as indicated by the teacher, e.g. *Formez un petit circle; Formez un grand carré*, etc.

Sports

Again this can be 'listen and do' or a guessing game. The teacher can call out sports for pupils to mime, or pupils can mime sports for others to guess.

Letter H

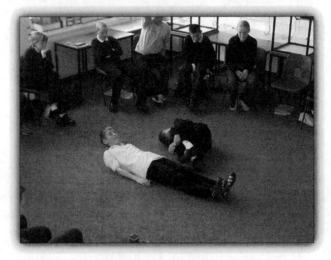

Number 10

Slow motion

A variation on the above. Students do their mimes in slow motion (*in Zeitlupe, au ralenti*). This requires better co-ordination and more concentration in order to mime as slowly as possible. It need not be restricted to sports. Students could for example be asked to dance a tango, or do the twist in slow motion. This activity is an excellent warm-up.

Musical instruments

The teacher calls out a musical instrument and students play that instrument. Alternatively, groups of students can form the shape of the instrument, and one student is asked to 'play' it. Eventually an orchestra/rock group/band of different instruments can be formed on the teacher's instructions. One pupil acts as 'conductor'. A melody is chosen and performed by the class, who mime and also sing in the manner of their instrument.

Walking on ...

The teacher tells the pupils to imagine that they are walking on different surfaces, e.g. ice, hot stones, mud, stinging insects, etc.

Miming to a story told by the teacher

You can devise your own stories. Exotic locations and unexpected events in an otherwise banal setting seem to work well. Here are some ideas:

- six people in a lift which gets stuck;
- lost in the jungle, hot, tired, you settle down to sleep – are woken by a snake dropping on you;
- people in a bank which is held up by robbers;
- at a disco/party – a famous pop idol suddenly walks in.

Port and starboard

This is a well-known Brownie/Guides' game. The following are the target language terms we use:

port	bâbord	Backbord
starboard	tribord	Steuerbord
land in sight	terre en vue	Land in Sicht
all hands on deck	tout le monde sur le pont	alle Mann auf Deck
raise periscope	sortez le périscope	Periskop 'rauf
captain's coming	voilà le capitaine	der Kapitän kommt
man overboard	un homme à la mer	Mann über Bord
the chef's gone	le chef s'en va	der Koch ist weg
the ship's sinking	le navire coule	das Schiff sinkt
here's the chef	le chef arrive	hier kommt der Koch
ship ahoy	navire en vue	Schiff ahoi

Ideas for group mimes (good for 'read and do' as well as extended 'listen and do'):

- Smugglers shifting goods.
- Members of a secret society moving crates of high explosives.
- Refugees loading possessions onto a cart.
- Removing a grand piano down a narrow stair.
- Toys in toyshop start to move at midnight.
- An ambush.
- Setting up camp.
- Astronauts assemble a space platform (slow motion).
- Divers clearing wreck under the sea.
- Thieves in the night, etc.

Miming and guessing

Using objects – 100 uses for a …
Teacher passes an object round the class. Each student in turn must think of a use for it and mime accordingly. The other students must guess in the target language what the object is supposed to be or what the student is using it for.

In the manner of …
Teacher prepares a list of adverbs on card. One student picks a card and must mime/carry out an activity chosen by the rest of the class in the manner of the adverb, e.g. open the door **furiously**, sing a song **passionately**, etc. The class must guess what the adverb is.

Statues/freeze frame
Groups of students think of a particular incident or scene, for example, a road accident, a rock concert, surgeons in an operating theatre, etc. They take up position and 'freeze'. Other students must guess what the scene represents.

One way of preparing this is to ask the students in their groups to think of a sentence or phrase which on its own indicates an entire situation, e.g. 'tickets, please', 'pass me the scalpel', and then to form the freeze frame.

Lost voice
Teacher prepares cards outlining a situation where things have gone wrong, e.g. your dog ate your homework, there's an elephant in the back garden, there's a snake in your bed, etc. One student picks a card and imagines that this has happened and that she has lost her voice. The student must mime in order to explain the situation to the rest of the class, who attempt to guess in the target language what is happening, until they arrive at the precise wording on the card.

FIND A PARTNER TECHNIQUE

This activity may be carried out either in a circle or in the normal classroom arrangement.

Basic technique

You need an even number of participants (teacher may have to join in if there is an odd number of students). Teacher prepares pairs of cards, which are shuffled and then distributed, one card to each student. Students are not allowed to show their cards to anyone else. Teacher informs students of the task in the target language (e.g. find the person the same age as you, find the answer to your question, etc – see examples below). Students move around the room trying to find their partner. This must be done by speaking in the target language and not by looking at other students' cards.

Find a partner

Once students have found their partner, they may:

* return to their own seats. Cards may be gathered in and activity repeated;

* sit down beside their partner and carry out a follow–up task (e.g. a conversation based on the topic on the cards);

* report back to the teacher, who can sort out any mistakes or problems.

The teacher should circulate among the students while they are attempting to find their partners and help out as necessary.

Eventually only a few students will be left standing. If they cannot match up their cards, then obviously a mistake must have been made. The teacher can then ask each pair to read out their cards, and check whether or not they have found the correct partner.

Varieties

Find your partner (ideas for cards)

Task:	Find someone with the same Christian name as you.
On cards:	Christian name and surname (e.g. Marc Dupont, Marc Leclerc, etc).

Task:	Find someone with two digits in their phone number the same as yours.
On cards:	Phone numbers (e.g. 44 64 22, 44 23 68, etc).

Task:	Find someone with the same pet as you.
On cards:	Pictures of pets.

Task:	Find the person who plays this sport/with the picture of this sport.
On cards:	Pictures of sports and sentences (e.g. tennis racquet and *Je joue au tennis*).

Task:	Find the person whose phrase, when combined with yours, makes sense.
On cards:	One half of a coherent dialogue (e.g. *Tu vas au cinéma demain?* and *Ah non, demain j'ai trop de devoirs*).

Task:	Find the sentence whose phrase, when combined with yours, makes a sensible sentence.
On cards:	Half a sentence each (e.g. *Mon frère a beaucoup de problèmes avec son prof de maths ...* and *... parce qu'il ne fait jamais ses devoirs*).

Task:	Find a person who is free at the same time as you and fix a date.
On cards:	Time of a possible date (e.g. *Lundi soir à sept heures and Lundi soir à neuf heures*).

Task:	You are a spy. You have to find your fellow agent who has the same secret codeword as you. You have to drop this word or phrase into a normal conversation otherwise the enemy agents will pick it up as they have 'bugged' the room. (NB you can do this with a large class where the students have to meet up with two or more agents to form a cell or network of spies.)
On cards:	A secret codeword or phrase (e.g. *étranger*).

Tips:

- Share the task of devising cards with colleagues and keep masters and cards centrally for all to share.

- Link what is on the cards to the themes or structures you are teaching. You can do this both to introduce new language or to practise what has been taught.

4 Simulations, improvisations and creative role play

There is a vast difference between role play as envisaged by examination boards and many textbooks, and the way in which drama teachers use this activity. Here we are looking at ways of engaging the imagination of the participants so that the language they use arises naturally out of the situation. The purpose behind the activities we are about to describe is not to practise particular structures, vocabulary or topics. It is to create a situation in which participants use language in a natural manner, as they would in mother tongue discourse. This is perhaps best illustrated by the following case study.

CASE STUDY 1: DEVELOPING A SCENARIO FOR THE TARGET LANGUAGE
Key Stage 4
Class S3 (in England Year 9) – 30 students of mixed ability

The students were asked in groups to think of a sentence or phrase that in itself summed up an entire situation. Someone chose *Passez-moi le scalpel!*, the latter word said hesitantly but with a French accent (we had taught our students to guess in this way rather than use English, and here, as so often, it was the correct word). The interaction with members of the class was as follows:

Teacher:	*C'est où?*
Student	*A l'hôpital*
Teacher	*C'est qui?*
Student	*Le docteur*
Teacher	*Plutôt chirurgien – et qu'est-ce qu'il fait?*
Student	*Une opération*
Teacher	*Qu'est-ce qui s'est passé?*
Student	*Il y a eu un accident!*

Other groups had similar fairly rapid exchanges to establish what they had chosen. From there all groups in the class made a freeze frame (see under 'Mime' p26) to illustrate their chosen sentence. The group mentioned above illustrated an operating theatre with each member of the team of four working out exactly how to stand/lie, etc, in their chosen role.

Other class members speculated on the situation – *Victime* was hazarded correctly; *Infirmière* was given in response to a request *Comment dit-on 'nurse' en français?*.

case study

The next step was to look back at how the victim had ended up on the operating table – *Il s'est fait écrasé?* from the teacher introduced a new construction which proved useful for a later expansion of the scenario.

The various groups moved back in time from their individual freeze frames. This group took as its starting point the moments just before the victim's arrival in hospital – general chit-chat between doctor and nurses, the bleeper announcing the arrival of the patient, preparation for the operation, etc.

This concluded that particular period and homework consisted of checking out any expressions they might need in order to develop their scene. Subsequent lessons developed the scenario, involving members of another group being co-opted to play the role of policeman at the accident scene, victim's family, etc. The whole drama and many of the scenarios which had arisen in other groups then became the meat of an improvised news bulletin which was 'run' in the course of a normal period, involving interviews, reports, etc, all filmed on camcorder. Not the tidiest of lesson plans – indeed there was no lesson plan, since the whole thing had its own dynamic which was under the control of the students themselves. But no-one was idle or bored and all of them were operating in French throughout.

Let's now look at a **creative role play arising from a stimulus** – you can use almost anything, e.g. concrete objects, a picture, sound effects, etc. These can spark off phone calls, paired role plays, group improvisations, storytelling, mime, acting out, etc.

Remember that drama is a **way of thinking** about teaching and learning!

case study

CASE STUDY 2: DEVELOPING CREATIVE ROLE PLAY FROM A STIMULUS

Class S5 (in England Year 12) – 20 students of good ability who have just read *Ein Anruf von Sebastian* which deals with relationships both within the family and between boy and girl.

The book ends on a decision by the girl to phone Sebastian some 18 months after they split up. As a result of changes she has made both in her life and her personality, Sabine now feels able to take the initiative and re-establish contact. (The details are in a sense immaterial – all books that we use now at this level deal with similar topics, if not exclusively, certainly contiguously.)

Telephone calls make a good starting point to a whole lot of scenarios. In this case students worked in pairs improvising the conversation between Sabine and Sebastian, whose characters they had already studied in some depth. From this to their next meeting the pairs stayed in role. Each pair envisaged their own 'ending', happy or otherwise, which they subsequently wrote up as a final chapter of the book.

Inventing role plays, improvisations and the like becomes relatively easy once language teachers abandon the notion of 'teaching the language' – i.e. vocabulary and structures of the language – as their only goal. Research into acquisition theory (Kraschen) and memory (Stevick) has been fundamental in our own reassessment of our teaching.

CASE STUDY 3: COMMUNICART: 3D ART AND LANGUAGE (JANET LLOYD)

The following flexible activity shows how another teacher, using drama techniques, introduces material not normally found in the languages classroom to stimulate learners' creativity, providing a basis for language production at a variety of levels.

It can be used to:
* investigate aspects of European art;
* explore a specific piece of art;
* develop spoken language to depict and interpret the story line of the picture;
* develop pronunciation and performance of language;
* develop the pose and presence of individual characters in the paintings;
* independently perform a role play depicting a specific scene;
* create the mood and atmosphere of a European city/market square/school yard through the sound of language;
* lead to a 'write up' and 'feedback' reporting session on what the observers witnessed.

The target group is either a KS2 Year 5/6 group (P6/7 in Scotland) or a KS3 Year 7/8/9 (S1/S2/S3 in Scotland) group. The teacher can guide the learners to the type of language that they can use, e.g. in Year 8 to utterances in the past tense (e.g. what have the characters just done/seen/eaten/drunk/played?) or in the future tense in Year 9 (e.g. what will these people do/eat/drink/play in the next moment or two?).

Alternatively, a combination of tenses could be used, or the activity could focus on simple utterances regarding a specific topic (e.g. clothes). Learners could express opinions and comment on what the others are wearing, keeping in character at all times. At KS2 utterances could be as simple as greetings or extended sentence answers, depending on the learners' ability.

You need:
* a one and a half hour/two hour drama workshop or three individual lessons;
* colour printed (laminated if possible) pictures of pieces of art that depict busy and interesting, potentially interactive scenes between people, or pieces of art where you need to decide what the people are thinking; these can be pictures by famous artists (e.g. Monet/Manet/Picasso), or pictures that visit a specific theme the class is currently exploring, or pictures chosen by the learners;
* a black and white OHT of each of the pictures which have been selected;
* personality cue cards.

Communicart plan

Stage one

1. Teacher divides learners into groups of four or five.

2. Teacher explains the role of art through the ages to depict events or make social comments on the time, and how performers would often retell important events through mime, song and drama .

3. Learners are asked to name artists they have heard of from different European countries and to explain what they understand about the type of art they produced.

4. Each group is given a black and white OHT of the piece of art that the group is to work on.

5. Pupils are given five minutes looking time; they can hold up the OHT to the light (at a window perhaps) and discuss the piece of art with their group. The discussion will depend on the group's ability. Teacher/learners should have prepared some simple questions in the target language, relevant to the picture, which can then be put on cue cards, e.g.:

How old is the character?
Quel âge a la vieille dame/le bébé/la fille/le garçon …?
Wie alt ist die alte Frau/das Kind/das Mädchen/der Junge …?

Where does the character live?
Où habite-elle/il?
Wo wohnt sie/er?

What is the character called?
Il/elle s'appelle comment?
Wie heißt sie/er?

How does the character feel?
Il est fatigué?
Ist er müde?
Elle est méchante?
Ist sie böse?

Describe the personality of the character.
Comment est la vieille dame/la fille/le garçon …?
Wie ist die alte Frau/das Mädchen/der Junge …?

These questions can vary in complexity and use of tense depending on the group's ability.

Beginners may like to respond with *'oui'/'non'* answers to questions prepared by the teacher and read out by a group member.

6. Learners take the role of someone in the picture and assume their pose. Other group members ask the individual questions in the second person singular.

Tu es fatigué? (Pourquoi?)
Bist du müde? (Warum?)

Question words in brackets are optional depending on group ability.

7. The group creates a still 3D copy (without speech) of the original OHT. Pupils could use props provided by the teacher specifically for the group, e.g. a hat/ a coat/a bag/a brush, etc. This will depend on the picture. Pupils could ask for props in French, German, using: *J'ai besoin de ...*, *Ich suche ...*

8. Teacher and other pupils look at each group's montage as if touring an art gallery.

Stage two

1. Teacher gives each group the colour print of their painting.

2. Groups are given five minutes to change their minds or develop the characters they have created, now that they can clearly see the artist's work.

3. Pupils practise the target language they intend to use, adopting the manner and imagined intonation of their characters. This can range from simple expressions like Hello (*Allô/Hallo*) / Goodbye (*Au revoir/Auf Wiedersehen*) / How are you (*Ça va?/ Wie geht's?*) / Please (*S'il vous/te plaît/Bitte*) and Thank you (*Merci/Danke*) to more complex structures, depending on level.

4. Learners now resume their poses in the montage and deliver their words/phrases in character.

5. There is now an opportunity for groups to view the 'art gallery' again, this time with a sound box, i.e. the other pupils in the class help develop a character's attitude and expression. They hear and see the characters speaking their phrases and the listening pupils agree/advise/support the characters in their poses and utterances. All pupils are viewing the actual colour picture at this time, enabling them to make informed comments. This can be followed by group feedback on how to develop the characters (with prompts from the teacher or in response to the teacher's questions).

    Tu es trop méchant./Du bist zu böse.
    Tu as besoin de .../Du brauchst ...
    Tu peux être .../Du sollst ... sein.

6. Back in working groups, learners discuss what they think is happening in the picture, with support statements or independently with dictionaries as required.

7. Learners develop the storyline of the picture (e.g. Who is the man?/Why does the woman look bored?/What is he afraid of?/Why is he hitting the baby?)

8. Pupils decide on phrases in the target language that best explains their own character's role in the picture.

Stage three

1. Learners practise as individual characters a specific action / series of actions that support and explain their character's utterance, e.g. 'I really can't tolerate her':

look at the person, throw back your head, turn and walk away/'Oh if only he'd love me': look adoringly at another character, put head in hands and smile at character, put hand on heart as if heart is broken.

2. Groups are given a time limit of fifteen minutes to produce a 3D portrayal of their group's piece of art, following the '3D art' rules: they must each speak in turn in an order that portrays the storyline of the picture, they must include actions to depict each character and they must consider how the character would deliver his/her own lines (intonation/inference/attitude/volume). Each character's actions and language should flow from one character to the next as in a moving picture.

Finally

Performances take place in the art gallery-style workshop, where all groups see the 'moving pictures' performed in turn.

The teacher can introduce an element of surprise and ask the groups to build the utterances into a round (as in music): the first character speaks, then the second starts while the first continues to repeat his/her own utterance, then the third character speaks while the first and second continue with their utterances, etc. The volume of the utterances gets louder and louder until all characters are speaking at the same time. Then one by one each character, in descending order of speaking, stops until only the first character is still speaking.

The teacher can explain or elicit from the pupils that this is what a market place/ continental school yard/street sounds like.

If a photo is taken at this point of every montage, the learners can develop a written feedback report (in groups or as individuals), describing the characters in the pictures or describing the storyline.

5 How do I get started?

▌ SOME HINTS AND TIPS

- Ask your drama colleagues for advice and help. Perhaps they might be able to team-teach with you?

- Ask your language colleagues/the FLA to take part in some co-operative teaching.

- Choose a class with which you already feel comfortable to start with. Remember that nothing succeeds like success! Once the pupils have enjoyed participating in one activity, they will be keen to try out another. Once you have had a first-hand experience of how much your pupils can get out of drama, you will be keen to try out other techniques and in particular try them out with other less motivated classes.

- Begin a normal lesson with a short 'warm-up' exercise (e.g.: 'Do you like your neighbour?' p14, 'Movement by numbers' p14, 'Beating time' p20, 'Mime' p23).

- Always stop an activity while the pupils are still enjoying it and asking for more.

- Teach your pupils to organise your classroom and how to move around in an acceptable manner (see under 'Movement' p22: 'Moving furniture').

* Bibliography

Halliday, M. (1975) *Learning how to mean: explorations in the development of language.* Edward Arnold.

Further reading

Brandes, D. and Phillips, H. (1990) *The gamesters handbook,* vols 1 and 2. Stanley Thornes.

Cumming, R. (1995) *Annotated art* (Annotated guides). Dorling Kindersley.

Dixey, J. and Rinvolucri, M. (1978) *Get up and do it!: sketch and mime for EFL.* Longman.

Hamilton, J. (1996) *Inspiring innovations in language teaching.* Multilingual Matters.

Hamilton, J. and Reid, S. (1991) *In play.* Nelson.

Hodgson, J. (1972) *The uses of drama.* Methuen.

Hodgson, J. and Banham, M. (3 vols: 1972, 1973, 1975) *Drama in education.* Pitman.

Hodgson, J. and Richards, E. (1974) *Improvisation.* Methuen.

Kraschen, S. D. (1992) *Principles and practice in second language acquisition.* Pergamon Press.

Maley, A. and Duff, A. (1982, 2nd ed) *Drama techniques in language learning.* Cambridge University Press.

McGregor, L., Tate, M. and Robinson, K. (1977) *Learning through drama.* Heinemann Educational.

Moskowitz, G. (1978) *Caring and sharing in the foreign language class.* Rowley MA: Newbury House.

O'Neil. C. (1977) *Drama guidelines.* Heinemann Educational.

Stevick, E. (1980) *Teaching languages: a way and ways.* Rowley MA: Newbury House.

Wagner, B. J. (1990) *Dorothy Heathcote: drama as a learning medium.* Stanley Thornes.

Way, B. (1967) *Development through drama.* Longman.

Selected resources

Gruneberg, A. et al (1997) *Atelier théâtre 1*. Macmillan Heinemann.

Kunz, D. et al (1997) *Theaterwerkstatt 1*. Macmillan Heinemann.

Treveri Gennari, D. et al (1997) *Dietro le quinte 1*. Macmillan Heinemann.

These titles constitute part of a suite of photocopiable resource books, originally written for EFL teachers, but translated into French, German, Italian and Spanish (the Spanish title is now out of print). This particular subset is designed to promote spoken fluency and takes the form of dramatic 'sketches', of four to five pages length, with guidance for teachers.

Domenech, M. G. (2001) *A escena, obras breves de teatro en español*. Spanish Embassy, Consejería de Educación.

Offers two pieces intended for younger learners, plus four appropriate for more mature students.

Oliver, C. (1996) *Kicking out*. ARC Theatre Publications (on behalf of Hockerill Anglo-European School).

Translation into French of a fully-fledged play (in 21 scenes), developed as part of a theatre-in-education project, addressing the issue of racism in football. Incorporates the playscript, plus an *appareil pédagogique*.

Nottinghamshire Education Committee, in conjunction with the University of Nottingham School of Education (1994) *Using drama in modern language teaching*. Nottinghamshire County Council.

Video (with manual) describing a one-day INSET programme, with contribution from a teacher who had previously attended, indicating its effects on her classroom practice. Contact Sue Craggs, tel: 0115 974 5575.

Part 2

With a song in my scheme of work

STEVEN FAWKES

WITH A CONTRIBUTION BY KHEYA MAIR

* Introduction

'... when a person endeavours to recall (...) he is like one who ascends a hill to survey the prospect before him on a day of heavy cloud and shadow, who sees at a distance, now here, now there, some feature of the landscape (...) touched and made conspicuous by a transitory sunbeam while all else remains in obscurity.'   W H Hudson

As teachers of languages we are constantly in search of sunbeams which will make the language we are presenting memorable to our class (and provide **us** with a feeling of well-being also).

The purpose of this book is to suggest some practical ways in which we can support learners of foreign languages at any stage in their learning and of whatever sort of ability by framing significant items of language in memorable formats, and by asking them to participate creatively in the work of the classroom. It focuses specifically on the creative context of song, but fits into the broader rationale for involving the imagination and a sense of style as significant aspects of language work.

The combination of familiar bits of language into new arrangements is an important language skill, and the impact of using such language in various situations and novel contexts serves the teacher in making the language involved more memorable.

All of the songs, scenarios and activities described below have been used in French (predominantly) and German classrooms where I have taught, some on many occasions and with different sorts of class, in comprehensive and special schools.

Two caveats at the outset.

- Not everyone responds well to different approaches. I think it is nevertheless worthwhile remaining optimistic, and giving things a try.

- What follows are activities which suit **me** as a teacher, which motivate **me** and which **I** enjoy planning and delivering. I hope colleagues teaching other languages or working on other topics will be able to make use of the underlying principles in their own teaching situations.

To those colleagues who are wary of their own ability to sing in the classroom, my experience is that the effect is not necessarily because it is done well, but because it is done at all.

1   Rationale: making use of the creative contexts

If one of the purposes of language learning is for personal use of the language in a variety of contexts, it follows that, from the outset, learners need **opportunities** to try out their language and gauge its effect; they also need empowerment through **confidence** to try to do something different with the language they know, in order to see it as 'more than a tool for functional/informational purposes' (as Carol Morgan puts it – *Language Learning Journal,* 1994); and they need **awareness** of a range of styles from which to select. The social competences of maintaining the flow of an exchange, entertaining people or just joining in are in need of development (or reinforcement) alongside the purely linguistic skills.

The judicious use of activities based on songs, games and drama may provide some of these opportunities by demonstrating:

- that a limited amount of language can make a big effect if framed properly; and
- that the little bit of language learnt can be used in more than one way and more than one context.

The principles of a multisensory approach are well established. A variety of learning styles exist; people respond to different sorts of approaches and resources, and teachers plan a wide variety of activities in order to interest the whole range present in classes, maintain motivation, keep attention and reinforce prior learning constantly in different ways. This applies particularly to less able learners whose attention span is often short, and yet who need a great deal of repetition in order to begin to internalise some of the core language they are presented with. The auditory route to learning can be reinforced through the involvement of rhythm, physical activity and tune which are all present in songs.

The strengths of using music to support language acquisition are particularly acknowledged in systems of Accelerated Learning, where the combination of relaxation, baroque airs and aural stimulus can produce significant memory gains. I would have to hesitate personally, however, before exposing my collection of J S Bach to the critical ears of a Year 9 class.

We learn that we can harness more of the brain's power by providing stimulus to its affective and creative hemisphere, by involving the personality, the imagination, music, movement and fantasy and by stimulating the limbic system through emotion and what is pleasing. This power can be invaluable in introducing language into the learner's short-term memory, where it can then begin to be processed by whatever language device the learner has available.

It seems that the brain's tendency to recall *'features of the landscape'* which are distinctive or unusual could and should be turned to our advantage as teachers. Just as we use visuals to present and recall target language words and expressions, so we can call upon the distinctive strengths of rhythm and music. In particular there is the area of language associated with music in the form of songs, rhymes and indeed jingles, as the hyperbole-manufacturers of the advertising world discovered long ago.

 ## A CONTINUUM

In encouraging the learners' personal involvement with the language we are learning, I hope, as a teacher, to develop three skills, by returning to them regularly:

 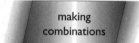 

In order to be able to participate at the higher levels of creativity and innovation, there seems to be some sort of continuum through which learners progress at different rates.

To support this progression, strategies can be identified by the teacher in the planning of lessons. Starting with the very basic level of willingness to participate,

this progression may include: ...   and examples of teaching strategies might be:

* being involved,   provide activities requiring participation;
* responding,   encourage interaction;
* guessing,   accept contributions of all sorts;
* personalising,   allow sink-in and thinking time;
* providing ideas,   demonstrate the brainstorming process;
* asking questions,   be open to queries and suggestions;
* experimenting,   be prepared to join in;
* extrapolating,   show that redrafting can improve on initial ideas;
* innovating,   provide a structure for pupils to work to.

For many of these strategies the use of a song or rhyme can provide an unthreatening context from which to begin. A song played on a cassette can, for example, be the basis for joining in, or for physical response, or for a collective brainstorm before developing words to a new verse.

There are significant planning issues connected with this continuum. Clearly, in order to be ready to participate in any sort of activity, we all need confidence that we can do so without embarrassment. The classroom atmosphere needs to be positive and imbued with the teacher's own willingness and conviction that what is going on is really interesting.

Many of the messages learners receive about what is expected of them, and what they in turn can expect, come from the general ambience of the classroom and the teacher's attitudes in managing the lesson. For example, as learners experiment with making suggestions or getting a feel for what sounds right in the language, they will make wrong guesses, of course. If such mistakes are not treated sensitively, there is very little motivation for anyone to try again. In order to feel supported, we all need to see the positive aspect of error, accepting wrong guesses not as mistakes, but as steps towards guessing better.

Within any sort of activity requiring people's ideas there is likely to be a requirement for reference skills, to avoid exhausting teacher-demand. At the same time, learners must be trained to use the things they know already (vocabulary, structures, communicative strategies) as the core of their invention, developing some sort of thought process in the target language; otherwise they will simply spend all their time translating their mother tongue ideas word for word with the dictionary, and end up with a hotchpotch of disparate words. This has implications for the amount of structure the teacher provides for learners in early stages of the continuum, the amount of time allowed for individual activities, and for the sort of training offered in coming up with other ideas, making new combinations of words, judging their effectiveness and choosing the best. Strategies for the teacher may include:

- suggesting zany/inappropriate ideas her/himself;
- gapfilling or redrafting activities done with the whole class;
- asking questions in order to identify alternative ideas and to gauge personal opinions and reactions;
- experimenting with creative hypothesis 'what if we change X to Y?';
- thinking about improving the quality of work, in terms of style or performance, as well as accuracy.

Again, the context of song has something to offer here, this time in supporting the teacher's confidence as well as that of the learners. With a personally devised stimulus there can, at the outset, be problems or worries about sensitivity. By selecting a pre-recorded song or a familiar tune for the class to work with, the teacher can more readily join in with the class in being critical of the original.

Using songs

The nature of a song or verse is that it is made up of sounds and of rhythm. 'Prose' language, as Monsieur Jourdain would call it, is made up of the same elements, but in a less structured format perhaps.

This suggests several ways in which the relationship between spoken and sung language can be supportive:

- We can put the rhythm into a spoken phrase, by clapping for instance.
- We can emphasise where the stress of a phrase lies, by humming its rhythm or by 'conducting' to highlight where the voice rises or falls.

This can be the basis for devising 'rap' phrases (or songs) which have many in-built repetitions, for consolidating purposes.

• We can additionally start from the song and pick out the rhythm of the language by repeating it.

Finally, and most significantly, songs are intended to be performed and to have an audience, key features of the communicative classroom.

2 Getting started

'Let's start at the very beginning, a very good place to start ...'

Performance requires an establishment of **confidence**, both on the part of the teacher and of the class.

In order to maintain confidence, whatever the activity, it is important to:

- have a good knowledge of the class and its dynamics;
- know exactly what you want to get out of the activity;
- have a good knowledge of the stimulus material;
- think about how the class will cope;
- be aware of the mood of the class, the mood of certain key individuals in the class and your own mood.

If the activity involves performance, it is also important to:

- plan for everyone to be busy, in one way or another;
- keep the performance activity short and provide immediate gratification;
- plan what will happen next, either as the follow-up or as the safety-net activity.

Instead of launching straight into activities involving songs for performance or other high-risk activities, it might be helpful to develop confidence and familiarity with this type of stimulus through a more steady progression. To start with, the class may be listening to the song stimulus, probably more than once, just as they may use a text from their course material:

- listening for key words, in order to match them with a list;
- listening in order to fill gaps in the text;
- listening in order to match the song to a multi-choice list of possible titles.

Gradually, the distinctive nature of the song-text can be developed:

- listening in order to review a song, maybe giving it a score out of 10 and a comment (see example below);
- listening in order to identify and then supply words which rhyme at the end of the lines;
- listening in order to identify and repeat the stress of a particular phrase;
- listening to pick out a particular group of words, for pronunciation training;
- listening in order to join in.

Different classes proceed through these stages at very different rates; some are keen to join in from the very first hearing, while others take a long time to be ready. This is one reason why a pre-recorded stimulus can often be much more satisfactory at the outset as it is much easier to rewind and replay, as well as reducing the threat of personal embarrassment by providing a backing track.

Once the class does seem ready to join in with a song, it is important to be realistic about how much they can cope with at a time, and what problems they may have with the lyrics.

The issue of presenting the lyrics themselves will depend upon the reading skills of the class. For many pupils in early stages of reading in a foreign language a request to read the written words, work out how they are pronounced and then reproduce them within the time constraints of a musical phrase can be very intimidating. In such cases it may well be helpful to choose a song with inbuilt repetitions, to focus on one particular phrase for the first rehearsal (or rehearsals), selecting a phrase which is fairly short, fairly frequent in the course of the song and, if possible, which forms a lexical item on its own. This can then be practised, using visual cues if helpful, before the musical reinforcement comes in.

An example from English could be …

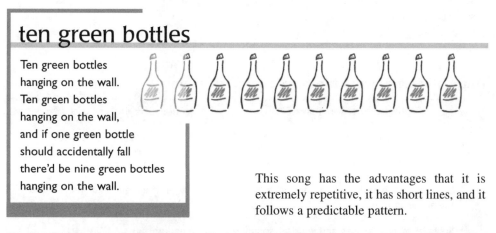

ten green bottles

Ten green bottles
hanging on the wall.
Ten green bottles
hanging on the wall,
and if one green bottle
should accidentally fall
there'd be nine green bottles
hanging on the wall.

This song has the advantages that it is extremely repetitive, it has short lines, and it follows a predictable pattern.

For the first hearing the key thing is likely to be the **rhythm** and one or two **sounds**. The second run through may pick out particular **words**, and for the first rehearsal you might select the whole **phrase/line** 'hanging on the wall', as it is repeated several times in the verse, is short, and is fairly complete in itself.

For the second rehearsal, you might take the line '*Ten green bottles*' itself, practise its pronunciation and then use visual clues to ask for ideas of how to say a change of number at the start of the line. During this rehearsal, the class can join in with part of nearly every line in the song.

Finally we are left with the filler-phrases and **the** difficult line, containing the polysyllabic 'accidentally'. This is where the rhythm of the song itself can support spoken skills as we can point out by clapping, tapping or conducting that the stress falls on the first and third syllables of the word, in order to fit the metre of the song. Thus learners have heard in this process that not only are there pronunciation rules governing individual words, but also that there is a certain intonation pattern to be expected when a group of words is put together.

When the whole of the verse is mastered by some members of the class, it can of course be extended into the verses which naturally follow it. Those who have not got hold of it all by now will have further opportunities to catch up during this extension period.

Once the teacher decides that a class is ready to move on to performance activities, the range of activities and of outcomes becomes rapidly much wider.

 ## WHAT SORT OF SONGS?

There is a variety of song material from which to choose according to the particular objectives we have for a specific class, and upon which we can build relevant activities, e.g.:

- authentic traditional songs from the target language country;
- authentic 'commercial' songs;
- purpose-written songs, linked to published resources;
- special, home-made songs;
- songs with actions;
- recycled songs, building on a model;
- rap.

Authentic songs from the target language country

What counts as a song?	Where do you get them from?
Children's songs, traditional songs.	Twin schools, friends' families.
Songs from records/cassettes.	Scavenging.
Songs from the radio, advertising jingles, theme tunes, raps.	Target language radio and television.
Songs in digital format and musical soundfiles. Clips of songs and samples.	The Internet.

Further sources of authentic songs are to be found closer to home in commercial publications, as well as in the broadcasts of educational radio and television programmes, and of course through networking with colleagues.

What are they like?

Before starting to search for such songs, we need to consider what we are hoping to get out of them any way, to establish whether the effort is worthwhile. As they are unlikely to fit particularly well into a language syllabus, it will be necessary to evaluate individual songs in order to judge their usefulness. An evaluation schedule is included in the Appendix (p86).

What are their strengths?

One of the listening skills pupils find most difficult to develop is that of ignoring the insignificant parts of a text they are listening to: they try to work out every single word they hear from the start, and end up frustrated and confused. As a way to put across at an early stage the concept that we do not need to translate or understand everything we hear, an authentic song could be a useful device. We do not, after all, have to worry ourselves needlessly about the rantings of the latest Heavy Metal group to enjoy (or otherwise) their performance.

Another strength of authentic resources lies in their great variety of style and of appeal.

The question 'Will the class like this song?' should be broadened to take in:

* Will it get a reaction from them?
* Will it illustrate something about the target language culture?
* Is there part of it that has something specific to offer?

LISTENING FOR PLEASURE

Real songs from other countries are usually very rich in cultural detail; everything from traditional songs associated with childhood to the titles in the current chart in a way form part of a nation's civilisation.

As songs are intended either for performance or for listening to, this implies that in the classroom we can use them as both speaking and listening resources. On the one hand they can be used for training people in pronunciation and rhythm by exposing them to the **flow of the song**. Encouraging them to join in and repeat **individual phrases or words** which are appealing can then support this awareness. On the other hand the very nature of musical composition is that it appeals to the emotions (and sometimes the intellect); it is often intended to be heard with pleasure, or to produce a particular response, such as the wish to move or dance.

This seems to have a particular contribution to make to the language learning environment, where, too often,

LISTENING = TESTING.

It could be that the inclusion into a lesson plan of some song material recorded from the radio or from a cassette for very short periods at fairly regular intervals would provide more of a link between –

LISTENING & PLEASURE.

In this case the listening activity would not be linked to the linguistic content of the song or necessarily to the development of oral skills; it would simply be, at the outset, 30 seconds or a minute of listening to something that other people like to listen to. Pupils could gradually begin to offer opinions on what they hear or make comparisons with other songs they know, but in essence this would be a break from the intensive flow of a lesson, possibly a settling activity between two stirring ones.

As such the role of these songs is quite different from that of **purpose-written songs** linked to published resources. Such materials contain songs, rhymes and other performance activities linked to the main language points developed in the resource and are now increasingly available. They are accompanied by activities and strategies for exploitation, and ideally reinforce the overall learning outcomes. (A brief list is included in the Bibliography on p89.)

A variety of possible exploitation activities is included in the following chapters.

LISTENING FOR PURPOSES

There are parallels between listening/responding to a song, and listening before producing any piece of spoken language, which are worth consideration.

For some learners the pace of lessons can be very difficult to cope with, and they sometimes do not spend much time being exposed to one set of language items before they are required to internalise and produce it themselves. It may be that the choral rehearsal of a song can provide a valuable midway point between passive and active participation.

In some ways the musical route from listening only to performance is much more supportive to the individual, as it takes things very much a step at a time. We have a fixed corpus of words we are going to produce; they are always in the same pattern; everyone else is producing the same thing in the same sequence. *'If I can't do it, the rest of the chorus will be there to buoy me up.'* With other forms of oral production the same structure is not available as the dynamics of linguistic interaction in pairwork, groupwork, classwork or individual communication are very much about dealing with the unexpected. *'I don't know exactly what I am going to have to say or what anyone else is going to say back to me.'*

At the point when the relaxed, receptive aspect of listening needs to be converted into the active, participatory aspect of production the problem of the unfamiliar language content of many authentic songs arises once again. Time is, after all, of the essence in a busy scheme of work. It is not only problematical to try to teach a new tune and new words at the same time, it is probably also inefficient to spend any significant amount of time on learning by heart a verse of which the language will not be obviously useful in other situations to be met later on, and one of the key words of our planning as teachers has to be **transferability**.

It is at this point that the home-made song comes into the repertoire, giving, as it does, control of the linguistic and grammatical content to the teacher.

HOME-MADE SONGS

The features of the home-made song are that it builds on what is likely to be familiar to the class anyway, both in terms of the tune 'borrowed' from some other context, and in terms of the vocabulary or other lexical items which they frame.

What counts as a home-made song?

- tweaked or recycled versions of children's or other songs;
- songs with actions;
- songs based on borrowed tunes: hits (probably of the past!), advertising jingles, theme tunes or traditional songs;
- raps and songs devised by the class, probably to a backing track.

Where do you get them from?

In order to recycle children's songs, it is a matter of taking the original, identifying the key foreign language words we can use to interpret it, and then fitting in other words to fill the gaps!

What are their weaknesses?

They require time for composition, refinement and conversion into classroom-based activities. They also require some imagination and lateral thinking, usually more available when there is more than one brain involved.

What are their strengths?

- the vocabulary and structures presented are purpose-selected;
- their tunes are already familiar;
- recordings are not always necessary. *A cappella* renditions mean that equipment is not needed;
- they are personal. They give the message that creative and entertaining things can be done with the functional or textbook-based language we have learnt together. If I can do it, so can they. (After all, I'm only a teacher.)

TWEAKING THE FAMILIAR

The attraction of editing childhood songs is partly in sending them up and partly in being prepared to participate in something which is recognised as being juvenile.

There is a certain amusement factor in using something familiar since infancy in a different way, as well as a considerable familiarity. The tunes are often wonderful, with lots of possibilities for repetition and personalisation. They are often associated with actions or movements, which can be used to great effect in supporting those (kinaesthetic) learners who need to move about to fix the language they are using.

The *Hokey-Cokey,* for example, is a song with obvious links to accompanying actions. This tune seemed to be ideal for recycling into practice of the language for 'finding the way' in German. The following example was for a class in their second year of German, familiar with the direction words, classroom language and vocabulary.

Ist das links?
Ist das rechts?
Links? Rechts?
Rechts? Links?
Ist das links?
In der Stadtmitte,
sprechen Sie lauter bitte!

Links oder rechts?
Oder was?
O bitte, bitte, bitte!
O bitte, bitte, bitte!
O bitte, bitte, bitte!
Links oder rechts?
Oder was?

Steps through the activity (each key item is accompanied by an action)

1. Setting the scene

'Ich bin in der Stadtmitte.' (I draw a circle with my finger and point at the middle. The class copies and repeats *'in der Stadtmitte.'*) *'Hier sind viele Autos* (mime), *viele Busse* (mime). *Ich suche die Schule. Hier ist eine alte Person* (mime). *'Bitte. Wo ist die Schule?'* (mime of dumbshow) *'Ich verstehe nicht. Ist das links?'* (left hand) *'Ist das rechts?'* (right hand) *'Oder was?'* (helpless hand signal) *'Ich verstehe nicht. Sprechen Sie lauter!'* (hand to ear mime) *'Bitte!'* (praying hands).

2. Presentation

Dictate the German phrases to elicit the correct actions from the class.
Perform each of the actions to elicit the verbal response from the class.
Ask individuals to recall the phrases in German to elicit the correct actions from the class.
Hum the tune.
Perform the actions in order. Try to fit the words to the tune.
Sing the song.

3. Performance

If desirable, the written words can be presented in order to improve the performance.

As for **songs based on borrowed tunes**, most of these are very individual, arising from the chance encounter of a concept or linguistic item, and a musical phrase. With practice, they can be searched for more methodically, and a bank of usable tunes can be put together.

It was after a performance of the *Hokey-Cokey* above that one of the class suggested we should do another one to a more modern tune and hit on the theme-tune to *Neighbours*. The assonance of the key-word with the German word *'neben'* ('next to' or 'near to') was striking, and it was soon evident that some other prepositions of place, which we had been learning, would fit with this tune, so eminently memorable that my greatest efforts to forget it are to no avail.

Steps through the activity

1. Introduction

Each of the prepositions has a movement associated with it. These have been used previously when we have met the prepositions in context. Here they are presented together orally.

Hört zu! Macht wie ich! Sagt was ich sage!		
WORD	**MEANING**	**ACTION**
auf	on	Hands on head
unter	under	Hands between legs
rechts	right	Point right
links	left	Point left
gegenüber	opposite	Hands point forward and back
vor	in front	Hands in front of chest
hinter	behind	Hands behind back
neben	next to, near to	Hands point to either side
zwischen	in between	Hands to either side of head

2. Linking with the written word

The words are revealed one at a time on the OHP, to encourage the class to read and respond with the appropriate action. They are read aloud for those who do not recognise the written form.

3. Linking with the spoken word

Pupils take turns to say one of the words; the rest of the class (including the teacher) does the required action; any errors in pronunciation are improved at this stage.

4. Performance

The words of the song are placed on the OHP. Hum the tune, or the introduction to the tune, and then sing the words accompanied with the actions.

5. Spin-off

Neben, *gegenüber, auf und neben,* *zwischen, hinter, vor und zwischen,* *auf und unter, rechts und links.*	*Neben,* *gegenüber, auf und neben,* *auf, unter,* *neben* *vor, rechts, vor links.*

When the prepositions are needed on future occasions, the appropriate action (with or without the tune) can jog the memory.

When might I use songs?

- for presentation;
- for practice or consolidation;
- for revision;

- for relaxation;
- for an injection of pace;
- to focus energy.

The question of how often to use songs is very individual to the response of the class and the pressures of a particular scheme of work. Clearly, the development of the cultural aspect of the language needs regular and frequent contributions, but these must be balanced against the language objectives and timescale in force. Ideally, the content of a worthwhile song will reflect what is in the syllabus anyway, and each topic will have an appropriate musical dimension, used for one of the purposes above.

Songs performed in class are often stirring activities; it is therefore not always right to use them at the end of a lesson, as this can disturb the class's departure. On the other hand, preparation is nearly always involved, so the start of the lesson is not appropriate either. Probably a good moment to move on to a song activity is when the class needs an energising moment, when they may start to be restless with other activities, and when there is still sufficient time to get started on a relevant follow-up activity before the lesson ends.

What can I do with songs?

In the continuing search for learning outcomes, the teacher finds possibilities in songs to:

- illustrate how rules of pronunciation work, and how they can be stretched sometimes;
- fix bits of language through the musical auditory route;
- develop purposeful, accurate copywriting skills;
- underline selected structures;
- encourage learning by heart (even if it is subliminal and in spite of themselves for some learners);
- encourage participation in the whole class, groups or pairs, through actions and through individual creation.

When they enter our classroom, pupils are immediately asked to believe themselves in another place, work and talk in different ways and develop tremendous enthusiasm for whatever the topic of the day is.

Building on the suspension of disbelief inherent in entering a foreign language classroom, as in the theatre, songs offer opportunities to the learners to:

- listen for (what might be a perverse sort of) pleasure;
- offer opinions;
- get used to the rhythm of the language;
- listen and respond in different ways;
- listen and repeat;
- perform and earn some applause;

but also at a higher linguistic level to:

• listen for a specific purpose;
• play around with words;
• predict according to rhymes or syllable count;
• extend or invent.

STRATEGIES

The strategies listed here are described with practical examples in the next chapter.

Skills	Strategies	Examples
Listening for pleasure	Reviewing	Awarding points to songs
Identifying pronunciation and intonation patterns	Rehearsing	(song 1)
Responding	Listening and doing	Physical response (song 2) Joining in (song 3) Sorting lines in to order (song 4)
	Performing	(song 5)
Linking sounds and writing	Following a text	(song 6)
Picking out detail	Checking a text	Amending verses of a song with a repetitive structure (song 7)
	Completing a text	Adding key words (song 8)
Remembering	Rebuilding a text	(song 9)
Developing a grammatical sense	Repetition of pattern Prediction	(song 10) (song 11)
Making a résumé or digest	Note-taking	Transposing the song into list of key words or phrases (song 12)
Inventing		(song 13)

3 My favourite hits

This is a digest of songs and accompanying activities, used for particular purposes with particular classes. The ages suggested relate to the National Curriculum years and are for guidance only; many of these examples have been successfully used with pupils of different age-groups also. It is my experience that the principles underlying these specific examples can be applied equally to different age-groups and different areas of language.

| **1** | **A song for pronunciation** | **Learners with some linguistic skill**
Year 9/10 |

Ta Katie …

The strategy here is to use the stimulus of the song to focus on particular sounds and their pronunciation, rather than the sense of the words.

This song by Boby Lapointe is an exhilarating tongue-twister in which the romantic misfortunes of Igor, abandoned by his girlfriend, are narrated by an alarm-clock. The language-level is very high, especially in the verses, but the chorus itself creates a splendid compulsion to try to imitate its pronunciation and rhythm:

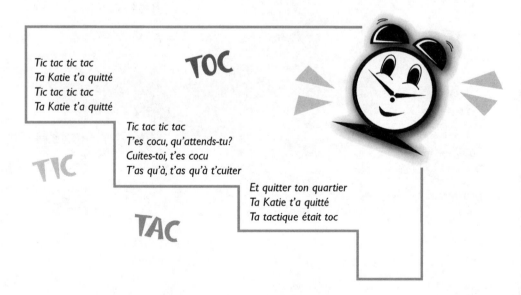

Tic tac tic tac
Ta Katie t'a quitté
Tic tac tic tac
Ta Katie t'a quitté

Tic tac tic tac
T'es cocu, qu'attends-tu?
Cuites-toi, t'es cocu
T'as qu'à, t'as qu'à t'cuiter

Et quitter ton quartier
Ta Katie t'a quitté
Ta tactique était toc

2 A song for physical response

Ça bouge

This is a recycled version of the childhood song 'One finger, one thumb …'. The strategy is to build up familiarity with key elements of the song gradually, using physical activity to support the new language.

It is important to remember that we do not need to respond to, or try to reproduce, the whole of a song, or even the whole of a verse straight away. This version of 'One finger, one thumb', for example, would be very difficult for a young class to get into directly. Consequently, learning such a song would need to be spread over several very brief sessions. In practice, at the outset, the focus of the first session could be simply on the refrain *ça bouge* accompanied by a rolling action of the hands; the relevant parts of the body and other actions could then come in gradually over subsequent sessions.

One advantage of a short physically active session such as this can be to refocus the energy of a class when their attention has started to dissipate towards the end of a long lesson. An extension activity can be for the class to suggest further actions which they can fit into the next verses.

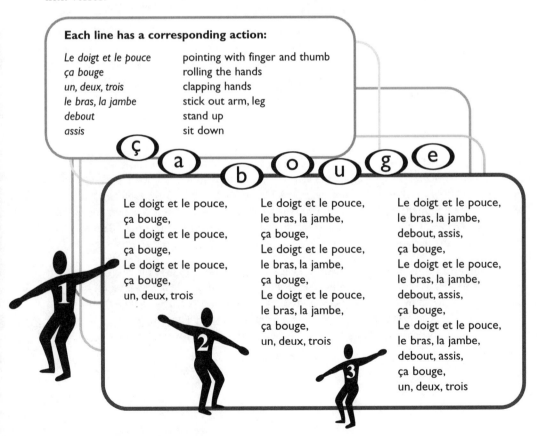

Each line has a corresponding action:

Le doigt et le pouce	pointing with finger and thumb
ça bouge	rolling the hands
un, deux, trois	clapping hands
le bras, la jambe	stick out arm, leg
debout	stand up
assis	sit down

Ç a b o u g e

Le doigt et le pouce,
ça bouge,
Le doigt et le pouce,
ça bouge,
Le doigt et le pouce,
ça bouge,
un, deux, trois

Le doigt et le pouce,
le bras, la jambe,
ça bouge,
Le doigt et le pouce,
le bras, la jambe,
ça bouge,
Le doigt et le pouce,
le bras, la jambe,
ça bouge,
un, deux, trois

Le doigt et le pouce,
le bras, la jambe,
debout, assis,
ça bouge,
Le doigt et le pouce,
le bras, la jambe,
debout, assis,
ça bouge,
Le doigt et le pouce,
le bras, la jambe,
debout, assis,
ça bouge,
un, deux, trois

3 · A song for joining in

Salut!

The strategy here is to recycle classroom language into a memorable framework, while at the same time suggesting that there are alternative ways of saying similar things. Thus the equivalences between *Comment vas-tu?* and *Comment ça va?* or *A demain* and *Au revoir* can be pointed out, with similar parallels in the mother tongue. As the amount of language is restricted, it has also proved successful with less able learners.

This song is in the style of the Seven Dwarfs from Disney's *Snow White*, to the tune of 'Hi-ho!'. It lends itself well to being linked to gestures and to being featured at the end of early lessons.

> *Salut! Salut! Salut!*
> *Comment vas-tu?*
> *Moi, ça va bien;*
> *donc, à demain.*
> *Salut! Salut!*

By nature of the original from which this borrowed, the verse then recycles itself until everyone has had enough.

4 · A song for sorting

Year 8

Hannibal

Songs are intended to be repeated or heard many times. One of the classic strategies for getting to know the parts of a conjugated verb is, of course, drilling; not everyone knows how to drill themselves and certainly not everyone is prepared to spend time on the necessary repetition. By treating the paradigm of a verb as a song, not only is there a context for a great deal of repetition, but also the usefulness of drilling, and some strategies, can be made transparent to the learners at the same time.

This example is for the present tense of the verb *avoir* and aims to drill the pronunciation of the words as well as their written form. The strategy here is to frame a verb paradigm, which the class needs to know and to note down, in a format which could help them to memorise it and provide a real reason for writing it down in the first place. The song is the end product of a series of steps intended to reinforce the language in different ways: use of visuals, aural discrimination and matching.

> *J'ai un chat, Hannibal.*
> *Tu as un animal?*
> *Elle a un chien.*
> *Nous avons des poissons.*
> *Vous avez des lions?*
> *Ils ont deux serpents longs.*
> *J'ai un lapin.*

Steps through the activity

1. Introduction

The visuals are presented on OHP or on a poster. The quality of the artwork is unimportant; indeed, the virtue of producing home-made, inaccurate drawings such as mine is that an initial activity can always be to spend some moments brainstorming in order to guess what they are intended to represent! (NB the significance of the speech bubbles and the gender and number of the characters is to relate to the personal pronouns subsequently.)

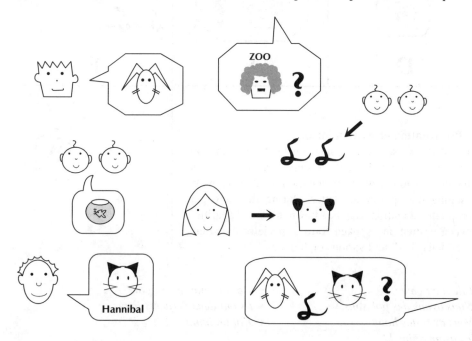

Different question types can be addressed in terms appropriate to the class or differentially to individuals in the class, in order to establish the vocabulary involved.

Plain question	*Qu'est-ce que c'est?*
Gapfill question	*Elle a un ...?*
Complex question	*Qu'est-ce qu'ils ont?*

Once the animal vocabulary has been rehearsed or presented, the visuals are shuffled into the order of the lyrics of the song. Each line is labelled with a letter to make the following matching activity straightforward.

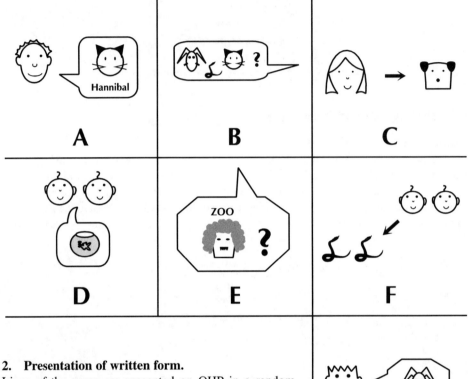

2. Presentation of written form.

Lines of the verse are presented on OHP in a random order; they are read aloud at the same time and the task of the class is to say which visual the line matches with, by stating the appropriate letter. During this stage, if appropriate, attention can be drawn to the disparities between written and spoken form, especially the silent 's', the liaised 's', and various diphthongs.

- *Elle a un chien.*
- *Nous avons des poissons.*
- *Vous avez des lions?*
- *Tu as un animal?*

- *J'ai un chat, Hannibal.*
- *Ils ont deux serpents longs.*
- *J'ai un lapin.*

3. Performance

Once the lines are arranged, it is appropriate to try to sing the song; it is in the style of the National Anthem.

The various rehearsals which follow provide useful drilling for the class, while the purposeful copying of the song into notebooks can include highlighting of the verb parts, and is consequently both a record of the paradigm and the stimulus for future performances.

<table>
<tr><td>**5**</td><td>**A song for performing**</td><td>**Young learners**
Year 5/6</td></tr>
</table>

 Gâteaux

This song was put together in a moderate learning difficulty school for a class of eight-year-olds who had been learning French for only a few weeks. Their curriculum was based on sweets and cakes as key motivating elements of their learning games and activities. The cross-curricular planning of their lessons meant that colours were high on their list of priorities as were numbers which they knew up to 8.

The main point of doing a song was to try to get them all involved in doing something together; secondary objectives were to do with recycling the vocabulary they knew, supporting their pronunciation and having fun.

This is to the tune of *Happy birthday* and was supported by the visuals on OHT. (NB the *e* on the end of *rouge* is enunciated.)

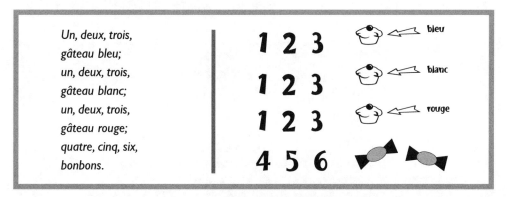

With a grammatical hat on, I could satisfy myself that at a first level the class had met the concept that adjectives of colour follow their nouns. In fact, they internalised this rule fairly naturally in that particular situation as the significance of the different colourings of cake relate to the school cook's predilection for icing the little buns she sent in at playtime with bright colours; this was language for a **real** purpose!

The children concerned were not in the least bit concerned with the word order, however. They **were** interested in the fact that they could later perform this song in assembly and receive applause for it.

Mon, ma, mes

Some tunes seem to offer themselves as frameworks.

My French classroom poster of possessive words looked like this:

A chance singing of the tune of *Frère Jacques* seemed to match this quite well but was not quite satisfactory. The modification of moving the first line to the end seemed to be a much neater arrangement, preserving the rhyme scheme better.

	le, l'	la,	les
Je	mon,	ma,	mes,
Tu	ton,	ta,	tes,
Il	son,	sa,	ses,
Elle	son,	sa,	ses,
Nous	notre,	notre,	nos,
Vous	votre,	votre,	vos,
Ils/Elles	leur,	leur,	leurs.

Mon,	ma,	mes,
ton,	ta,	tes,
son,	sa,	ses,
son,	sa	ses,
notre,	notre,	nos,
votre,	votre,	vos,
leur,	leur,	leurs,
le,	la,	les.

Savez-vous …?

Using a traditional song such as *Savez-vous planter les choux?*, a simple listening activity is built around the idea of editing the first verse according to what is heard in the subsequent verses. This can be done using visuals, using cards with the keywords written on them (*nez, pied, main,* etc) or as a gapfilling activity.

(Chorus)	*Savez-vous planter les choux*
	à la mode, à la mode?
	Savez-vous planter les choux
	à la mode de chez nous?

(Verse 1)	*On les plante avec **le nez***
	à la mode, à la mode
	*On les plante avec **le nez***
	à la mode de chez nous.

(Verse 2)	*On les plante avec **le pied***
	à la mode, à la mode
	*On les plante avec **le pied***
	à la mode de chez nous.

In each verse the part of the body changes; after a few examples, the class can begin to make its own suggestions about words they could substitute for those in bold, and then perform these verses to see how they sound.

8 A song for completing   Year 8/9

Shirley Bassey

When pupils are used to handling the written word, they can be asked to manipulate the words of a song as a listening activity. This particular example is a tribute to Shirley Bassey and can be performed with all the glitter and razzamatazz associated with that singer.

Steps through the activity

1. Introduction
This activity is intended to revise some of the vocabulary and functions connected with a visit to the café. It uses the written form of words on a *'carte de boissons'*, but tries to inject a sense of style into the subject by framing the language in a glitzy context. The activity begins with study of the 'carte', and the association of the words with flashcards.

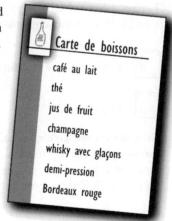

2. Participation
The task is that of a collaborative performance. The teacher is the singer; the class is the band who have to sing the introductory bars in order for the performance to start. The context is that I, the teacher, am the waiter in a café, addressing a female customer, and recommending a range of *'consommations'*.

3. Listening and putting in order

The first stage of building up the lyrics for the song is for the class to hear the verse sung through, and to organise the drinks on the 'carte' into the order in which they are heard. This should be checked after the first or second run through, so that the next stage can be done effectively. At this point, the task is to take the functional bits of language presented here and sort them into the order they take in the song. The contribution of the class as musicians pertains.

> *vous voulez*
> *peut-être*
> *s'il vous plaît*
> *Mademoiselle*
> *voilà*
> *entrez*

4. Joint performance

If the class is very participative, they may wish to perform the song for themselves now. In any case, extension activities can build on the performance. A second verse can be devised, either in toto or in order to complete, from a list of potential rhymes supplied, a verse such as the following. In this instance the customer responds; this second role can be taken by a member of the class, if they are confident enough.

> *'Mademoiselle, entrez, s'il vous plaît.*
> *Voilà!*
> *Vous voulez …? Un jus de fruit?*
> *Un champagne?*
> *Un Bordeaux rouge?*
> *Whisky avec des glaçons?*
> *Un café au lait?*
> *Peut-être du thé?*
> *Un demi-pression?'*

To the tune of 'Hey, big spender!'

1. *'Mademoiselle …'*
2. *'Monsieur, s'il vous plaît.'*
3. *'Comment?'*
4. *'Je ne voudrais rien à manger, ni à boire.'*
5. *'Mademoiselle …'*
6. . . . .

Some interesting suggestions for a final line have included the romantic: *'Voulez-vous sortir ce soir?'* and the surreal *'Donnez-moi une pêche et une poire!'*.

Further extension activities can include producing a cartoon version of the song, or writing a script with accompanying stage instructions.

9   A song for rebuilding   Year 8/9

La matinée

Building on the combination of actions with words and tune, more elaborate linguistic formulations can be framed. The following activity presents those reflexive verbs most commonly needed for talking about the daily routine. As the verses needed to be fairly lengthy to fit in the several syllables of the verbs, a popular school hymn suggested itself.

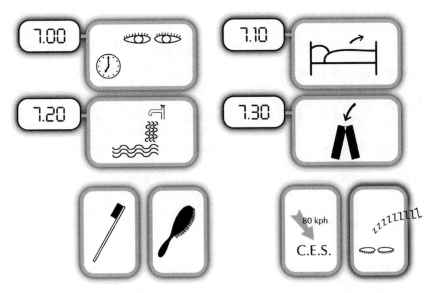

So, in the style of Ancient & Modern, this is to the tune of *Lead me O thou great Redeemer*.

> *A sept heures je me réveille.* *Je me brosse ...*
> *Sept heures dix et je me lève.* *Je me brosse ...*
> *Sept heures vingt et je me lave.* *Je me dépêche en classe et ...*
> *Sept heures et demie et je m'habille.* *Maintenant, je suis fatigué!*

Steps through the activity

1. **Introduction**
   - Presentation of visuals on OHP and drilling of the related language item: *Je me réveille; Je me lave*; pupils suggest associated actions.

   - Practice of recognising the language items; pupils perform the actions.

   - Personalisation stage: pupils respond to a visual on the OHP by saying the phrase and adding something to it, if possible. *Je me réveille ... à sept heures et demie. Je m'habille ... dans la chambre.*

   - Presentation: Recapitulation of telling the time, using a digital clockface on OHP.

   - Sample recombination of visuals of time with the other visuals. Pupils practise saying a longer phrase.

   - Asking for ideas: The visuals are placed one by one on the OHP. Pupils suggest appropriate times to accompany them. This is extended by adding a visual of the Mr. Men character Mr Topsy-Turvy (Monsieur Alenvers). The task now is to provide entirely inappropriate ideas!

2. Preparation of the song

Visuals are placed in the appropriate combination for the words of the song on the OHP; pupils provide the words of the song, line by line, matching it with actions as appropriate.

3. Whole class performance

4. Follow-up

Using the visuals as a prompt, pupils write a draft of the verse, alone or in pairs. This is then checked by a dictation process. Pupils dictate to the teacher what they have written for each line. The teacher transcribes on to the board or OHP, asking for spelling as appropriate and concentrating on significant details, such as reflexive pronouns or unsounded letters. A second draft can then be written up.

 A song for grammar   **Year 8**

 Pommes

The history of this activity lies in a request to devise a song which would present to a Year 8 class examples of the grammatical rule that *ne … pas* is followed by *de* instead of *du, de l', de la,* or *des*. The scheme of work indicated that the vocabulary for this should be 'fruit', as presented in the coursebook. The consequence was a potential whole new area of experience: 'The world of having no fruit'!

Steps through the activity

1. Introduction

'On va préparer une chanson ensemble.' The first stages of this twenty minute part of a lesson were to check on vocabulary of fruit (with flashcards and realia) and to present examples of the structure in context. To this end we imagined a fairly bizarre situation: I was in the market, my basket was depicted on the OHP, and someone from the class was putting fruit into it. As I was facing away from the screen, I could only guess what was in the basket by asking the class:

'J'ai des fraises?'	*'Non.'*
'Je n'ai pas de fraises. J'ai du raisin?'	*'Non.'*
'Je n'ai pas de raisin.'	

2. Groupwork

We then introduced *Tu as …* and moved on to a group activity based on this same information gap exercise. Pupils invented their own basket illustration, and their group took it in turns to identify the appropriate item.

3. Discovering the words

The visual cues below were placed on the OHP, and volunteers suggested what they thought the corresponding lines of the song would be.

4. Recording in writing

A particular concern with this class, as with many others, was their inaccuracy in writing. This showed itself particularly in small, but frequent, mistakes involving *Je* confused with *J'ai*, and omitting the letter *s*. For this reason I asked the class to write down the words **with me,** i.e. watching me form the words on the screen, and keeping pace. I wanted to point out particular things as they occurred, and to avoid swamping the poorer readers with the whole text in one go. So, as they dictated the lines to me, I wrote them up ...

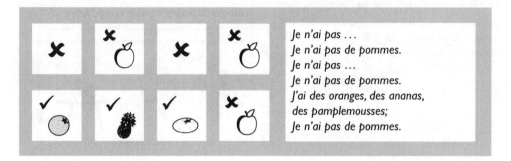

When completed, we went through the following sequence. I hummed the tune to them once, hummed it again, pointing to the words in time, and then sang the verse through. It is a tribute to the football terraces and has the tune of *We shall not be moved.*

5. Invention by extension

The task of the class in the last few minutes of the lesson was to work in pairs to devise a new verse to this song. During this session the classroom was buzzing with people drilling themselves frantically, as they tried things out. *Je n'ai pas de ..., Je n'ai pas de ..., Je n'ai pas de ...*

Examples

Je n'ai pas Je n'ai pas de pêche Je n'ai pas Je n'ai pas de pêche J'ai des cerises, des bananes et du raisin Je n'ai pas de pêche	Je n'ai pas Je n'ai pas de prune Je n'ai pas Je n'ai pas de prune J'ai des poires, des bananes et des melons Je n'ai pas de prune

6. Further extension

As the song went down well, it returned from time to time throughout the year and was passed on to other colleagues. Much later on, I met one teacher who told me her class had had considerable fun doing the same activity with 'clothes' vocabulary. Their favourite chorus had been: *Je n'ai pas de slip*!

Another example of extension

The extension activity does not need, of course, to relate exactly to the song-context from which it springs. With another class who learnt this song, pressure of time suggested it would be appropriate to consolidate the recognition of the pattern *ne ... pas + de* by setting a short written homework activity. For this, a new Mr Men character was invented and illustrated in a cartoon. *Voici Monsieur Napas.*

The homework task was to create another cartoon about Monsieur Napas, using the same structure, for display on the classroom noticeboard.

Monsieur Napas regarde Neighbours ...

... mais il n'a pas de télévision!

11   A song for prediction   Year 10/11

 Paulette

This activity exploits the features of rhyme and syllable count within a verse. It is really for older learners, to rehearse rules connected with the perfect tense and to involve people in coming up with ideas and making suggestions.

Steps through the activity

1.   Introduction
The verse is on OHT. ' *Voici un vers. Il y a des mots qui riment.*'
An example of rhyming words can be given to ensure the concept is clear.

2.   Presentation
The verse is revealed, and read aloud, line by line on the OHP; the words marked with stars are covered up with slips of paper and only revealed when they are correctly identified. '*J'ai mangé chez Paulette; j'ai pris ma* ∗ ∗ ∗ ∗ ∗ ∗ ∗ ∗ ∗'. When the hidden words are reached in the text, a syllable count can help to suggest an appropriate word. Suggestions can be stored on the board for a follow-up activity, or just for comparison with the original. Some of the gaps to be filled are nouns; the articles preceding these gaps are useful cues, reminding learners of basic elements of grammar to do with gender. Other gaps are verbs, or parts of verbs, and the process of filling the gaps can focus on their formation, including the agreement of the past participle.

A table!

<table>
<tr><td>

(Version on OHT)

J'ai mangé chez Paulette;
j'ai pris ma * * * * * * * * *
choisi sauce tomate
avec mon * * * * * * * * .
J'ai mis la moutarde
et la mayonnaise;
j'ai bu du sirop –
du sirop à la * * * * * * .
J'ai pris ma serviette;
j'ai dit 'Bonne * * * * !'
Sur mon assiette
j'ai vu une * * * * !
Je l'ai dit à Paulette
et elle a crié.
J'ai été surpris;
mon assiette est * * * * * * !
Cette bête (à trois * * * * *)
a * * * * * mes frites.
Je me suis levé,
mon sirop est * * * * *,
et je suis parti tout de suite!

</td><td>

(Complete version)

J'ai mangé chez Paulette;
j'ai pris ma serviette,
choisi sauce tomate
avec mon omelette.
J'ai mis la moutarde
et la mayonnaise;
j'ai bu du sirop –
du sirop à la fraise.
J'ai pris ma serviette;
j'ai dit 'Bonne fête!'
Sur mon assiette
j'ai vu une bête!
Je l'ai dit à Paulette
et elle a crié.
J'ai été surpris;
mon assiette est tombée!
Cette bête (à trois têtes)
a mangé mes frites.
Je me suis levé,
mon sirop est tombé,
et je suis parti tout de suite!

</td></tr>
</table>

Follow-up

This verse is sung to the tune of Julie Andrews's *My favourite things*. Nearly all of the final *e*s are voiced. The words can alternatively be learnt or read as if they were simply a poem or tongue-twister. The text can also be transposed from first to third person, to see if the same rhythm can be retained. The alternative suggestions stored on the board can be used to make up new verses to the song, either in class or at home.

La famille Vabien

This is sung to the tune of *Auld lang syne*. The words are as follows:

> *Anne est la mère;*
> *c'est Pierre, le père;*
> *des deux enfants Vabien,*
> *La fille est Claire;*
> *le fils, Robert,*
> *et Bruno, c'est le chien.*

However, before reaching the stage of hearing the song, I would like the class to help me assemble the lyrics using visual prompts, so that we can then use the same prompts to sing it subsequently, without having the interference of the written form of the words. Furthermore, at the end of the activity session I want them to use the visuals and a variety of reference items to record the words of the song accurately. Firstly, I want to reinforce the differences between *le* and *la* words in order to remind them of that most difficult concept, that everything has a gender in French.

For this I use a simple 'sorting sheet' on the OHP, like this:

m.	f.

Steps through the activity

1. **Introduction**
   i. *'On va faire une chanson sur une famille. C'est la famille Vabien. Voici Pierre, Bruno, Anne, Claire, Robert.'*
   Show the names on the OHP, one at a time.

   ii. Put the pictures, one at a time, onto the OHP. Pupils guess which name goes with the picture, in order to practise pronouncing the names.

   iii. Grammatical section. *' Pierre est le père de la famille. C'est Monsieur Vabien. Anne est la mère. C'est Madame Vabien.'*
   Use the 'sorting sheet' to place Pierre's picture in the 'Masculine' box; then Anne's into the 'Feminine' box. Do the same for the children of the family, teasing out a response from the class as to whether your choice of box is correct. The class should now have visual support for grouping the *le* words together and the *la* words together. The question of where to put the dog now arises! Hopefully the cue word **le** *chien* will be sufficient to guide the class to the right conclusion about its gender.

(This same activity can subsequently be extended and reused for any vocabulary set just to keep reminding people, when they are thinking of a word for *the,* they do have a choice to make.) The sorting sheet is kept available for the end of the activity session, when the class takes its own notes.

2. **Building up the lyrics**
'Comment s'appelle la mère? Et le père? Et la famille? Il y a combien d'enfants? Comment s'appelle la fille? Et le fils?' The class has now heard the key language several times and a quiz should allow the words to be put together in the right order. When the correct answer is forthcoming, the teacher confirms it with the appropriate line of the song, i.e. *'Comment s'appelle la mère?'* *'Anne'* *'Oui, Anne est la mère.'* In this way the verse is put together. It works quite nicely if the last line is not presented until the first performance to the tune, at which time there is a certain satisfaction when the lyrics actually fit!

3. **Performing the song.**
The tune is introduced simply by humming it. Personally, I like to perform the song first by myself with the class joining in if and when they can, but that stage can possibly be omitted. Depending on the class, their recall of the song may be stimulated solely by the visuals, if it is rehearsed enough; otherwise, the written form may need to be presented beforehand.

Pronunciation skills: there is always a risk of interference when pupils read with their non-French-speaking eyes and speak accordingly, but sufficient unscripted preparation beforehand can be coupled with specific attention to difficult letter combinations and words (*c'est*, *enfants*) in order to raise awareness of the conventions of French pronunciation.

4. Follow-up

The issue of following up a song activity is dependent on the class and their response to the song. In order to get the most out of our training with *le* and *la*, the class should now make their own notes on the song, using key words, e.g. '*Anne – la mère, Pierre – le père*' etc.

However, alternative plans are sometimes required with different sorts of classes.

- Some groups might be asked to copywrite the whole verse at this stage.
- Another group might like to make a class recording.
- For another group further questioning provides a brainstorming activity about the characters in the song. '*Quel âge …?*' '*Qu'est-ce qu'il/elle aime faire?*' etc, which leads into a creative writing activity.
- For yet another group the task is for pairs to come up with either a new verse to the song, or a verse about a different family.

 A song for adding ideas   **Year 8**

 Gegenüber der Disko

In order to begin to test what they can do with the language they know, learners need to begin from a supportive structure, with enough of a framework so that they can see what is expected of them. There are few things more intimidating than a blank page and instructions to fill it!

The following activity involved pupils in putting in new ideas into a preordained structure. It is quite a short activity that fitted into a sequence of other approaches within a lesson to do with German prepositions and their cases in the context of places in town. The largest part of the lesson was taken up with:

Whole class stage:

- OHP presentation of visuals;
- presentation of words, and matching with visuals;
- manipulation of visuals, using prepositions (*rechts von dem Rathaus*);
- spotting the links between the preposition and the sound of the article following it (*neben der Post*);
- trying to predict the link;
- looking at the written form of the words.

Pair work stage:

- jigsaw activity with the written forms (*neben der +?*);
- information gap activity based on a town plan.

Individual work:

• reading activity based on the same language;
• writing activity based on the same language.

In order to change the context, and to draw the class back together, a tribute to Judy Garland was introduced based on a blackboard picture. It is to the tune of *Somewhere over the rainbow*.

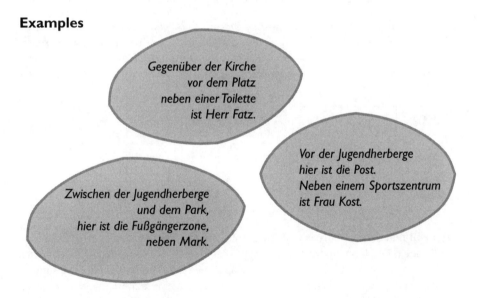

Gegenüber der Disko,
vor dem Park,
neben einer Toilette
hier steht Mark.

In order to move into an idea-suggesting stage, this verse requires a very specific brainstorming session; after all, there are only a limited number of people's names that actually rhyme with the names of places in town!

Examples

Gegenüber der Kirche
vor dem Platz
neben einer Toilette
ist Herr Fatz.

Vor der Jugendherberge
hier ist die Post.
Neben einem Sportszentrum
ist Frau Kost.

Zwischen der Jugendherberge
und dem Park,
hier ist die Fußgängerzone,
neben Mark.

Case study: Using melodies and rhythm as a tool for teaching foreign languages (Kheya Mair)

Why is it that the melody and lyrics of a song suddenly come back to you, years after you first heard it? Could we as language teachers try to employ similar strategies to enable our students to recall simple or even complex sentences in the target language?

It has been remarked that pupils retain sentences for a longer period of time if they learn them with the help of a simple tune.

For example, asking your class to memorise and reproduce the line:

'Moi, j'habite à Wallasey près de Liverpool qui est située dans le nord-ouest de l'Angleterre ... et ça me plaît.' ... would seem a little daunting to the average Year 7 pupil – until you start a 'knee-clap, knee-clap' background beat while scanning these words to *'House of Fun!'* by *Madness.*

Moi,	j'ha-	bite	à	Wall-	a-	sey ...
Wel	come	to	the	house	of	fun ...
Knee		clap		knee	clap	knee ...

You will find that not only is your class chanting the line in unison, perfectly in time with each other, but you, the teacher, will be able to dictate the speed of the sentence by slowing down/quickening the pace of the 'knee-clap' pulse. Without the support of the background beat, this would be a difficult whole class activity to control, given the length of the sentence. Supplying your pupils with the written word will cater for the visual learner and smooth out any pronunciation problems as they exercise their reading, listening and oral skills at the same time. The aural/oral learner is also being stimulated (through the melody/rhythm) as is the kinaesthetic learner (through physically clapping and keeping a beat.)

case study

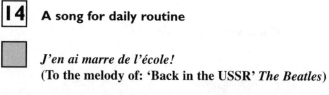

J'en ai marre de l'école!
(**To the melody of: 'Back in the USSR'** *The Beatles*)

I wrote this song with the topic of 'Daily Routine' in mind, but one of my aims was to combine vocabulary specific to this theme with language associated with '*Mon Collège*'. I also wanted all pupils (top set Year 8) to commit the whole song to memory, a task which they found challenging but at the same time rewarding as they eventually managed to do this after two lessons (followed by a learning homework!). Three years on, many of these pupils remembered lines from this song and were able to fit them into their GCSE oral examination! This is how I would teach the song.

As the beats of the bar (shaded on the illustration on p76) are quite difficult to scan, pupils could begin by **numbering the four beats** of the bar, as shown on the illustration. Pupils and teachers should be aware that these four beats will sometimes run from one line into another. While the (*) symbol denotes a rest in the bar (the number accompanying it denoting the respective beat of the bar), it would be better to sound this with a clap. These strong beats will act as landmarks enabling pupils to feel more focused and centred for the following game!

After the melody and rhythm have been introduced, pupils can be taught the French lyrics concentrating on one line at a time. This is to be done by clapping out the syllables and then saying the words in the same rhythm. The pupils echo this and should very quickly be able to say line one at speed and use the same rhythm as the teacher.

Next, establish how many syllables are contained in each line. For example, **line one holds eleven syllables** up to the comma. Now tap out the rhythm of these eleven syllables, stopping suddenly at various points. Depending on whichever syllable you stop at, the class have to predict the **following word**, e.g. if **four beats** are sounded by the teacher, the pupils would be expected to say '*je*' as their answer, as this is the **fifth** syllable in line one. This method encourages accelerated learning as pupils are focused on the sound and spellings of each word at the same time. Support can be slowly taken away by asking your class to turn over their sheets. Repeat the spoken exercise but now ask them to **write** down the next word. This promotes accuracy and tests pupils' knowledge of the written word. Pupils will quickly realise that certain words have more than one syllable and therefore, if they were to hear two beats sounded, they would have to write the full word '*matin*' to gain a mark as opposed to just '*ma*'.

case study

J'en ai marre de l'école!

1   2   3   4
Lundi matin, je me lève à sept heures trente, puis
1   2   3
je vais à la salle de bains. (*4)
1   2   3   4
Je me douche et ensuite je me brosse les dents
1   2   3
Je mange du toast, je prends le train
     4   1
… Pour aller à l'école, (*2) (*3)
     4   1   2
J'en ai marre de l'école, moi … (*3),
     4   1
J'en ai ras le bol! (*2) (*3) (*4)

1   2   3   4
Normalement, j'y arrive à huit heures et demie,
1   2   3
Parfois je suis en retard, (*4)
1   2   3   4
Jacques fait ses devoirs d'anglais qu'il n'a pas fini, car il
1   2   3
Sors avec Nicole tous les soirs
     4   1
Je n'aime pas sa Nicole, (*2) (*3)
     4   1   2
Je la trouve un peu fol-le! (*3)

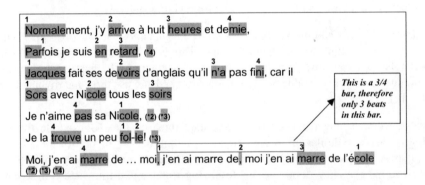

This is a 3/4 bar, therefore only 3 beats in this bar.

     4   1   2   3   1
Moi, j'en ai marre de … moi, j'en ai marre de, moi j'en ai marre de l'école
(*2) (*3) (*4)

1   2   3   4   1   2   3
Son premier cours, c'est français, suivi par l'histoire, (*4)
1   2   3   4
Et moi, ce que je ne peux pas supporter, c'est
1   2   3   4   1
Histoire-géo, E.M.T, sciences et surtout faire mes devoirs! (*2) (*3) (*4)

A song for describing your area   **Year 9**

Qu'est-ce qu'il y a près de chez toi ?
(**To the melody of: 'When I'm 64'** – *The Beatles*)

I wrote the lyrics to this song as a consolidation activity after having taught the theme of '*Ma région*' to a Year 9 set. This song would lend itself to group or pair work as it is in the form of a conversation and contains two different 'voices' (black and grey in the example opposite). The final aim for the pupils would be to sing the words off by heart! The pupils in this set achieved this after a 40-minute lesson and a large number of them performed the song (with actions!) in assembly and at the 'Wirral Festival of Languages' where they were awarded first prize.

The song could be exploited in many ways. A logical place to start would be to play the original Beatles song to your class which would remind or introduce them to the **melody.** At the same time, **scan the pulse** with your class, i.e. clapping along to the strong beats of the bar. There should be four claps/beats to each bar.

Now show the **French lyrics** to your pupils and see if they can clap out each syllable, emphasising the strong beats (shaded in the illustration on p78) with louder claps or nods. Once they have mastered the rhythm of one line, slowly introduce the lyrics aurally, making sure you stick to the identical rhythm. (The pulse may be played throughout by the teacher using a tambourine or bongo drums!)

I would do this as a whole-class repetition exercise, taking one line of French at a time.

(NB: The word '*retrou-ve*' should be sung as three syllables in order to rhyme with the word '*Louv-re*'. The symbol (*) denotes a rest and is the fourth clap/beat of the bar in this song.)

Pupils can now be split into two groups. Half of the class would sing the **black** lyrics and the other half would sing the **grey.** The words in **capitals** are to be sung together.

Groups one and two would then swap over before the whole class attempts the full song with (then without!) the aid of the teacher.

As a follow-up lesson to this, teachers could hand out the worksheet on p78 which promotes **comprehension** of the text while guiding pupils with **pronunciation.** Pupils are to unscramble the text by numbering the lines 1–7 in the boxes. (The first line of each verse is already numbered and the last line of each verse is underlined). While placing these in the correct order, pupils should be encouraged to see/hear how certain vowels look and sound through **rhyme.** Finally, they could be asked to find the rhyming scheme.

(E.g. this would be **AA-BB-CC-DD-C** for **verse 1** and **AB-CC-DD-EE-D** for **verse 2.**)

With a little support, this could lead to pupils composing their own songs in French!

case study

Card 1

Qu'est-ce qu'il y a près de chez toi?

- — Non, je les trouve ennuyeux!
- 1 — Dis-moi, qu'est-ce qu'il y a près de chez toi?
- — On se retrouve devant le Louvre
- — Est-ce que tu aimes regarder les films d'horreur?
- — Ce que j'adore, c'est les comédies Car elles me font rire (ha, ha, ha)
- — A sept heures et demie!
- — Il y a un cinéma …

- — Ça fait des années que je n'ai pas nagé pourtant c'est mon sport préféré
- — On se retrouve devant le Louvre
- — A midi moins vingt!
- — Prenons le bus comme c'est assez loin,
- — Il y a une belle piscine. (CHOUETTE!)
- — N'oublie pas ton maillot de bain! (WHOOH!)
- 1 — Dis-moi qu'est-ce qu'il y a près de chez toi?

Card 2

Qu'est-ce qu'il y a près de chez toi?

- — *Dis-moi, qu'est-ce qu'il y a près de chez toi?* (group 1)
- — Il y a un cinéma … (*) (group 2)
  Est-ce que tu aimes regarder les films d'horreur?
- — *Non, je le trouve ennuyeux!* (group 1)
  Ce que j'adore, c'est les comédies
  Car elles me font rire (ha, ha, ha)
- — On se retrouve (group 2)
- — *devant le Louvre* (group 1)
- A SEPT HEURES ET DEMIE! (*) (together)

- — Dis-moi qu'est-ce qu'il y a près de chez toi? (group2)
- — *Il y a une belle piscine.* (group 1) (CHOUETTE!) (together)
- — Ça fait des années que je n'ai pas nagé (group 2) pourtant, c'est mon sport préféré
- — *Prenons le bus comme c'est assez loin,* (group 1)
- — N'oublie pas ton maillot de bain! (group 2) (WHOOH!) (together)
- — *On se retrouve* (group 1)
- — devant le Louvre (group 2)
- A MIDI MOINS VINGT! (*) (together)

5   Let's do the show right here!

 LEARNERS INVENTING

There can be many purposes to which the stimulus of a song or verse can be put in the classroom, and the same stimulus can be used equally well with younger pupils or the less able as with older pupils or the more able if the activity associated with the song is challenging at an appropriate (cognitive) level.

Although invention of pieces of language in a song format can be seen at the end of the line of progression, this line can be shorter or longer, depending on the support provided. Learners can be led into inventing or creating their own verses and songs at various levels, from *'arrange these lines into a sequence you like'* through *'substitute new words (or lexical items) for those highlighted'* towards *'produce a verse of your own'* and even at this level the difficulty of the task can be varied to suit the situation:

* invent to fill a gap (either at the level of individual words, or of a whole line);
* invent to extend;
* invent to imitate the format of the stimulus;
* invent to fit a certain length of the line (for a collaborative effort, for instance);
* invent to fit the metre pattern;
* invent to fit a rhyme scheme;
* invent to fit a tune;
* invent a verse on a topic;
* invent in a particular style (e.g. a radio jingle).

The nature of the work produced can also be focused by the objective of the activity:

* inventing in order to publish will produce the need for an accurate piece of writing;
* inventing in order to perform will produce the need for fluency and clear articulation;
* inventing in order to record will produce the need for high quality voices and probably accompaniment.

 AU CAFÉ

A class of Year 8 pupils was learning about going to the obligatory café in France. In order to get them to try out new combinations of words and rehearse pronunciation, the tune of *Old MacDonald* proved very useful in providing a new context for their practice language, and for putting in new ideas.

Steps through the activity

1. Introduction

This was set up as an anecdote using as a prop an extremely stale croissant. *'J'entre dans le café. Je dis bonjour. Le garçon arrive.'*

'Monsieur? Vous désirez?' 'Je voudrais une tasse de café, s'il vous plaît.'

'Avec un croissant?' At this point the displeasing aspect of the croissant is made extremely apparent.

'Non, merci. Une tasse de café.'

'Avec un croissant?' There follows a great deal of repetition and some farce. Symbols are placed on the OHP to stimulate recall of the words.

2. Performance (NB The *e* of *une* and *tasse* are enunciated).

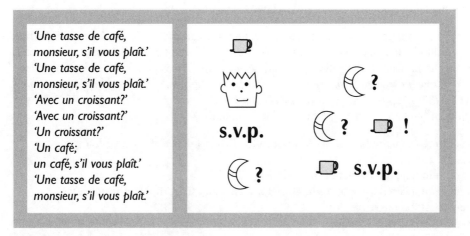

'Une tasse de café,
monsieur, s'il vous plaît.'
'Une tasse de café,
monsieur, s'il vous plaît.'
'Avec un croissant?'
'Avec un croissant?'
'Un croissant?'
'Un café;
un café, s'il vous plaît.'
'Une tasse de café,
monsieur, s'il vous plaît.'

3. Follow-up

i. Applause is required. The supportive atmosphere of the classroom needs to operate in all directions.

ii. The symbols are used for the class to perform the song, firstly in chorus, then with different groups taking the roles of the customer and the waiter.

iii. A whole-class brainstorm session makes some initial suggestions for a second verse. Different food and drink items can be tried, along with other ideas; observations on how a suggestion sounds are made at a very basic level, and alternatives can be tried out. By humming the tune and counting on their fingers, pupils can begin to think about syllable-count.

iv. In order to liberate those pupils who can cope with a less rigid structure, a hypothesis is introduced to those groups: *Dans le café, il n'y a pas de garçon; il y a une fille ...* They suggest what changes will need to take place accordingly.

v.   A few minutes only are spent with a partner coming up with a new verse. This activity needs to be brief to avoid the problems of ideas becoming too elaborate or of dictionary interference.

Examples

A pair of girls opted for the waitress in their café, necessitating a complete redraft, as *Mademoiselle* takes up more space than *Monsieur*. Their refrain was:

> *'Mademoiselle, s'il vous plaît.'*
> *'Une tasse de thé.'*

A pair of boys presented me with their paper upon which was written the single word 'bière'. Taking my puzzled silence for expectation they went straight into a rendition:

> *'Une biè-è-è-è-re,*
> *Monsieur, s'il vous plaît.'*

Perhaps this counts as 'Differentiation by outcome'?

RECIPE FOR A HOME-MADE SONG

1.   First catch your tune. Open a file on memorable tunes that may come in handy some time.

Familiar tunes (if possible lousy ones; they're less threatening and more memorable) include:

i	Childhood tunes:	very flexible as they tend to be repetitive.
ii	Songs from the shows:	the big film musicals offer lots of inspiration.
iii	Hits of the '60s, etc.:	rhythmic and upbeat.
iv	Carols and hymns:	depending on the background of your school.
v	Tunes from the TV:	adverts and theme tunes are designed to be memorable.

Examples

i	
	Ten green bottles
	Old MacDonald
	Auld lang syne
	Twinkle, twinkle, little star
	Three blind mice
	Charlie is my darling
	One man went to mow
	She'll be coming 'round the mountain
	Greensleeves

ii	
	White Christmas
	Climb every mountain
	Supercalifragilicexpialidocious
	Singing in the rain
	(or almost anything sung by Julie Andrews)

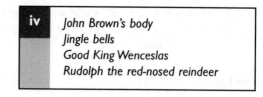

iii	She loves you Sailing Yesterday Yellow submarine

iv	John Brown's body Jingle bells Good King Wenceslas Rudolph the red-nosed reindeer

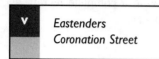

v	Eastenders Coronation Street

2. Secondly, choose between the inspirational route (2a) or the task-solving route (2b).

2a. Look/listen for any assonance between a word in the original and a key word in the target language. Look also for conceptual links. Sometimes a pattern in the first line of the song makes a lateral connection with a phrase in the target language and starts the words flowing into their framework.

2b. Decide what parcel of language you want to frame in a song. Look/listen for a tune with the right sort of syllable count per line. Think of possible alternative wordings you can use, in case the original phrase proves problematical. When fitting words into the framework, be flexible. Without compromising rules of intonation, pronunciation and syntax, it is often possible to find a different order of words or change the selection of words slightly to reach a more satisfactory conclusion. Be prepared to abandon a cherished phrase if it just won't fit. Look for possibilities of rhyming words.

Example

The task was to find a way to present the articles *au, à l', à la, aux* with examples in a memorable framework.

i.   The hunt for a song with similar sounds in it led from *à l'* to *The Alleluia Chorus*.

ii. A list of possible examples was compiled: *à l'église, à l'école, au garage, aux magasins, au syndicat d'initiative, à la mairie.*

iii. Looking for rhyming words suggested that *garage* would benefit from *plage* and *village* as rhymes.

iv. Fitting the words to the tune indicated that many of the musical phrases are quite short (4 beats) but also highlighted the need for one very long phrase linking the verses.

v.   Trial and error led to the decision about which lines to make rhyme. After manipulating the possibilities for a while, there seemed to be a state when the verse felt all right. It can later be amended in the light of experience of course.

The first verse ended up so:

> *A la plage;*
> *au garage;*
> *à l'école;*
> *au village;*
> *à la gare.*

with the final *e* enunciated once again.

There were more examples to be incorporated, however, and the class could cope with a broader vocabulary base than this. A variation produced a new verse with some more difficult combinations of sounds:

> *A la plage;*
> *au garage;*
> *à l'agence ...*
> *de voyages;*
> *à l'hôpital.*

This was where the long phrase was needed (10 beats). Which places might fit here? *A l'Office de tourisme* was too short, as was *au Syndicat d'initiative*. Fortunately, the police station came to the rescue with its syllable count and its intonation intact:

> *Au commissariat de police;*
> *à l'église;*
> *à l'église;*
> *à l'église;*
> *à l'église.*

The National Library has a different intonation pattern, meaning that the *la* needs to be slightly swallowed to keep the flow going:

> *A la Bibliothèque Nationale;*
> *à la piscine municipale;*
> *à la piscine municipale.*

It's then back to the same short format lines as above:

> *A la plage;*   *A la plage;*
> *au garage;*   *au garage;*
> *à l'agence ...*   *à l'école;*
> *de voyages;*   *au village;*
> *à l'hôpital.*   *à la gare.*

There is a sense of intellectual satisfaction when everything seems to fit in its place. However, the problem in practical terms turned out to be that not very many of my pupils were well up on their Handel. (See 'Beware' below.)

Bear in mind

- The less new language you include, the more digestible the song will be, the more impact it will have on first hearing, and the more rapidly it can reach performance.

- The first bit of a tune is very flexible; for example, you can always hum yourself an introduction if your words don't start until halfway through the line.

- In French it is a convention that the *e* which is usually mute on the end of a word can be enunciated at the end of a verse, if it helps.

- If the musical line is too long, you can make one syllable last for several notes, but this sounds odd unless it is a significant syllable. For example, it sounds all right to stretch the main syllable of a word like *trente*, but not the *e* at the end.

- You will want to exploit the impact the song makes straight away; what sort of follow-up will be appropriate?

- Do you want to link lyrics with actions or visual cues, or make the link with the written word clear?

- How will the song activity fit with your classroom practice?

Beware

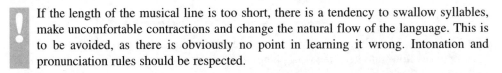

If the length of the musical line is too short, there is a tendency to swallow syllables, make uncomfortable contractions and change the natural flow of the language. This is to be avoided, as there is obviously no point in learning it wrong. Intonation and pronunciation rules should be respected.

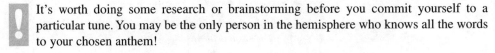

It's worth doing some research or brainstorming before you commit yourself to a particular tune. You may be the only person in the hemisphere who knows all the words to your chosen anthem!

PLANNING PRINCIPLES

Appropriateness
Pace
Accessibility
Practicability
Mixed skills
Expectations
Enjoyment

- There are times when the introduction of a song activity is particularly appropriate. Any sort of excess or imbalance is to be avoided!

- The audience for the type of activity outlined above tends to thrive on a mixture of familiarity and variety, and performs best in activities which are **short** enough to be accomplished within their attention span. The issue of **pace** within a lesson also comes into play here.

- Any activity must be unthreatening (for teacher and pupils) as well as **clear and accessible.** If there is any risk of people getting lost, by accident or design, this has to be remedied.

- It can be clarified by identifying **clear objectives** for the activity. This helps teachers know what they want (listening for pleasure or for review, joining in, writing down, adapting or inventing) and helps them stay within the limits of what is achievable in the time available.

- The principles of **mixed skills** apply here as elsewhere in activity design; there should be opportunity not just for hearing or singing a song, but also for following it up, building on it, or extracting something from it.

- A word about the teacher's own performance: the reaction of individual classes to different sorts of approaches is fairly unpredictable, however, it is probably best to **expect** some laughter if you burst into song unexpectedly. This is partly from surprise, partly from embarrassment, but is really part of the game and should be built on as a positive stimulus for further enjoyment. Teachers uncomfortable with singing themselves frequently could make use of a backing tape (with or without the words) to support the activity.

  Similarly, there are things to **expect** about the performance of the class: reading the words and saying or singing them is hard, as two processes are involved at once. The use of short lines, visual clues and much drilling can be anticipated.

- Finally, the major principle behind all the preceding is that of enjoyment, looking for angles on what needs to be done anyway, in order to put it across in a way in which learners and teachers can share a sense of pleasure in one aspect of the manifold uses to which people put language.

Appendix

EVALUATION SCHEDULE

In the interests of making effective use of classroom time, the following schedule may be useful in focusing attention on the merits or problems of using a particular song.

(NB As I am the person who is going to have to present the song to the class and carry them along with my own enthusiasm, I put my own opinion at the top of this list! Clearly, if the answer to questions 2 or 3 is 'No', the song will go into the decent oblivion that awaits all exhausted *Eurovision* entries. If the song does make it on to the lesson plan, I will need to ascertain the response of the class afterwards, of course.)

Song title:_____

1 What is this song like?_____

2 Do I like it?_____

3 Will class X like it?_____

4 Will another class like it?_____

5 When does it seem to fit into the scheme of work?_____

6 Will I use all of it?_____

7 When will I use it in the lesson plan?_____

8 What will I use it for?_____

9 How will I use it?_____

10 What will the learner/teacher gain from this?_____

Example

Quand trois poules vont aux champs,
La première va devant;
La deuxième suit la première;
La troisième vient la dernière.
Quand trois poules vont aux champs,
La première va devant.

	Song title: <u>**Quand trois poules vont aux champs**</u>	
1	What is this song like?	Jolly
2	Do I like it?	Yes
3	Will class 7A like it?	Yes
4	Will another class like it?	?
5	When does it seem to fit into the scheme of work?	Unit 8
6	Will I use all of it?	Yes
7	When will I use it in the lesson plan?	End of lesson
8	What will I use it for?	Confirmation of ordinal numbers, place words
9	How will I use it?	Visuals of hens, numbers to manipulate on OHP, play tape, join in
10	What will the learner/teacher gain from this?	Bit of fun

Example

Vive le vent, vive le vent,
vive le vent d'hiver
qui s'en va en courant
dans les grands sapins verts.
Vive le vent, vive le vent,
vive le vent d'hiver.
Boule de neige,
grands sapins blancs
et bonne année, grand-père.

Song title: __Vive le vent__ (tune of 'Jingle bells')

1	What is this song like?	A bit difficult
2	Do I like it?	Yes
3	Will class 8B like it?	Maybe
4	Will another class like it?	Y7, other Y8
5	When does it seem to fit into the scheme of work?	Christmas
6	Will I use all of it?	Yes
7	When will I use it in the lesson plan?	Start of lesson, end of term
8	What will I use it for?	Mainly for pleasure, maybe some pronunciation work with more able groups
9	How will I use it?	'-ent', '-in, '-ant' sounds
10	What will the learner/teacher gain from this?	Cultural reference

Bibliography

Collins, E. (1995) *Le français, c'est facile!: French songs for special educational needs*. John Murray: supports Brown, S. and Dean, S. (1995) *Le français, c'est facile!: strategies and resources for special needs*. John Murray.

Elston, T., McLagan, P. and Swarbrick, A. (1995) *Génial*. Oxford University Press: uses a regular Karaoke feature on its cassettes.

Jenkins, B. and Jones, B. (1992) *Spirale 2*. Hodder and Stoughton: set of three cassettes accompanies the book; cassette C is *Spirale musicale*.

'Ta Katie t'a quitté' words and music by Boby Lapointe, 1964. © Editions musicales INTERSONG TUTTI, 74, bd de la gare, 75013 Paris.

Selected French resources

Bourdais, D., Finnie, S. and Gordon, A. L. (1998) *Equipe*. Oxford University Press. An audio-CD containing all the songs from this course is available separately.

McNab, R. (1999) *Métro* (Books 1 and 2). Heinemann. Each module features a song, included on the cassettes.

Song cassettes published by **MGP/Stanley Thornes**:
Chanterelles
Chantez OK!

BBC Television series regularly include authentic and purpose-written songs. Examples:
Jeunes Francophones
Quinze minutes plus
Hallo aus Berlin
D-Mag

www.wanadoo.fr has a section *'Infos et loisirs'* and a link to *'Musique'*. It also offers live Internet links to a range of French radio stations.

www.alapage.com is commercial (something like Amazon) but contains sound clips from albums from the catalogue, as does the FNAC site: **www.fnac.com.**

www.francealacarte.org.uk, the French Embassy website, gives access to **www.french-music.org,** which then leads on to sites of specific musicians.

For information on contemporary music resources contact: Bureau des musiques actuelles, Institut français, Queensberry Place, London.

The above list is necessarily selective, but a wide range of 'songs' packages for language learning are now available, intended for varied audiences (notably, but not exclusively, learners of primary age). Details are included in some CILT information sheets; you are also referred to the catalogues of major languages booksellers and distributors.